Cambridge Studies in Ethnomusicology

The Dastgāh *Concept in Persian Music*

The tradition of Persian art music embodies twelve modal systems, known as *dastgāhs*. Each *dastgāh* represents a complex of skeletal melodic models on the basis of which a performer produces extemporised pieces. These unspecified nuclear models are no more than broad outlines which guide the combined arts of performance and composition.

It is a personal and illusive tradition of great subtlety and depth. Through extensive research, including interviews with leading musicians and recording over one hundred hours of music, Hormoz Farhat has unravelled the art of the *dastgāh*. In his study, Farhat analyses the intervalic structure, melodic patterns, modulations, improvisations within each *dastgāh*, and examines the composed pieces which have become a part of the classical repertoire in recent times.

Cambridge Studies in Ethnomusicology

General Editor: John Blacking

Ethnomusicological research has shown that there are many different ingredients in musical systems. The core of this series will therefore be studies of the logics of different musics, analysed in the contexts of the societies in which they were composed and performed. The books will address specific problems related to potential musical ability and practice, such as how music is integrated with dance, theatre and the visual arts, how children develop musical perception and skills in different cultures and how musical activities affect the acquisition of other skills. Musical transcriptions will be included, sometimes introducing indigenous systems of notation. Cassettes will accompany most books.

The *Dastgāh* Concept in Persian Music

Hormoz Farhat

Professor of Music
*School of Music, University of Dublin,
Trinity College*

Cambridge University Press
*Cambridge
New York   Port Chester
Melbourne   Sydney*

PUBLISHED BY THE PRESS SYNDICATE OF THE UNIVERSITY OF CAMBRIDGE
The Pitt Building, Trumpington Street, Cambridge, United Kingdom

CAMBRIDGE UNIVERSITY PRESS
The Edinburgh Building, Cambridge CB2 2RU, UK
40 West 20th Street, New York NY 10011–4211, USA
477 Williamstown Road, Port Melbourne, VIC 3207, Australia
Ruiz de Alarcón 13, 28014 Madrid, Spain
Dock House, The Waterfront, Cape Town 8001, South Africa

http://www.cambridge.org

First published 1990
First paperback edition 2004

A catalogue record for this book is available from the British Library

Library of Congress cataloguing in publication data
Farhat, Hormoz.
    The *dastgāh* concept in Persian music / Hormoz Farhat.
        p.   cm. – (Cambridge studies in ethnomusicology)
    Based on the author's thesis (Ph.D.) – University of California at Los Angeles. 1965.
    Bibliography.
    Includes index.
    ISBN 0 521 30542 X hardback
    1. Dastgāh.   2. Music – Iran – History and criticism.   I. Title. II. Series.
ML344.F32   1990
780′.955 – dc20 89–15704 CIP

ISBN 0 521 30542 X hardback
ISBN 0 521 54206 5 paperback

To the memory of my son
Kāmrān

Contents

Preface

Although I am of Persian birth and have lived my childhood and teenage years in Persia, my early musical outlook was mainly western. I remember some fascination with Persian music in my childhood when, on rare occasions, my father played the *tār*. He was an amateur musician who, like most nobility of the time, had learned how to play an instrument in his younger days. But from the coming of radio to Persia, I found myself much more drawn to western music. The first radio station was established in Tehran in 1939. Local musical broadcasts included both Persian and western musics. It was the popular western songs and dances (tangos, waltzes, foxtrots, etc.) which were more commonly heard, but there was also a limited broadcasting of classical recordings.

I was first drawn to the likes of 'La Comparsita', 'J'attendrai' and 'The Blue Danube'. From there I moved up to the *Caucasian Sketches*, *Scheherazade* and the Second Hungarian Rhapsody. The next step was to Grieg, Tchaikovsky, Beethoven, and so on. As my interest in western music grew and turned into a passion, what little place Persian music had within me was given up altogether. By the time, in my late teens, that I had decided to devote my life to the study of music, I had no feelings for Persian music other than contempt. As compared with the wealth, variety and range of expression in western music, Persian music seemed limited, frail and monotonous.

Several years later, having already completed a B A in Music at the University of California at Los Angeles and an M A in Composition, under Darius Milhaud, at Mills College, I returned to U C L A, to embark on study and research towards a Ph.D, and came in contact with Mantle Hood. Then, in 1955, he had just been appointed an Assistant Professor in the Music Department and was about to begin building a programme of ethnomusicological studies which rapidly, by the mid-sixties, became the most extensive in all American universities. It was Mantle Hood who eventually persuaded me to do my doctoral research on Persian music. I was initially disinclined to do so as I continued to regard Persian music – most non-western musics, for that matter – with some derision. However, I could not resist Hood's argument that the musical heritage of such an ancient and distinguished culture as that of Persia must possess qualities of value and interest, and I could not fail to appreciate his point that being a native of that culture I am inevitably better equipped to grasp those qualities than a non-Persian. Furthermore, I was compelled by the suggestion that a study of Persian music, about which next to nothing was known, would constitute a more valuable contribution to musical knowledge than a research on an aspect of western art music, very little of which remains obscure.

Soon after settling on the aim of a definitive research on Persian classical music, I realised that a firsthand field study was necessary as there was hardly any material worthy of research available in the U S. In the 1950s, as yet, no book or article of any sort had been published, in western languages, on Persian music. I was fortunate to receive a Ford Foundation Fellowship and returned, after eight years in the US, to my native land in 1957.

In Persia, I carried out extensive research for two years on the urban musical tradition. My approach to the study of the music was both practical and analytical. I took regular lessons in *setār* (long-necked lute) and *santur* (dulcimer). I collected whatever publications that were useful to my study and worked at several libraries. I interviewed most of the leading musicians of the old school and recorded more than one hundred hours of music. These recordings proved to be the most useful aspect of my research. In time, I was able to transcribe much of this recorded music into western notation for the purpose of study and analysis, a work which continued for a number of years after my return to the US in 1959. The thesis for my Ph.D, based on this research, was finally submitted in 1965, when the degree was conferred.

By this time my earlier misgivings about Persian music had been replaced by a deep appreciation of its unique aesthetic qualities. I no longer compared it, consciously or unconsciously, with western art music. It is a very different musical expression. It is monophonic; it employs a range of sound generally not exceeding two and a half octaves; it is fundamentally soloistic but not virtuosic; and it lacks grandeur and dramatic power. But it is rich in modal variety, in melodic subtlety, and is highly personal and intimate.

Since my first research, conducted during 1957–9, I had occasion to do further studies on Persian music, particularly in the period 1968–76 when I was back in Persia involved with various academic and educational projects. The present book is mainly the thesis of 1965 which has been in some respects revised. I remain convinced as to the conclusions reached then which have been reconfirmed by my more recent contacts with Persian music.

Both at the time of my original research, and in my more extended stay in Persia during the 1970s, I benefited from the friendship and help of many of the country's leading musicians, some of whom are no longer living. I must pay particular homage to the memory of Ruhollāh Xāleqi, a noble and learned musician, who gave me much help and guidance in my early studies. Also, I remain indebted to the generosity of the late Nasrollāh Zarrinpanje, who taught me a great deal, including how to play the *setār*. My *santur* teacher and gracious friend was Hoseyn Sabā who died when quite young. My grateful thanks also go to many others, including *Ostād* Ahmad Ebādi, *Ostād* Farāmarz Pāyvar, *Ostād* Asqar Bahāri, *Ostād* Jalil Šahnāz, Mehdi Meftāh, Zāven Hacobian, and all those who by the virtue of being the inheritors and the guardians of the treasury of Persian music, have been the instruments of its survival, most of whom I have known as good friends or worthy associates.

I must also express my appreciation to my dear and respected friend and colleague, Professor John Blacking who has given me the needed encouragement to submit this work for publication. My thanks also go to Miss Caroline Gillespie for her assiduous help in the typing and printing of the musical examples.

Note on transliterations

In the past few centuries countless books have been written on Persia in various European languages. However, Persian words and names, when their use in a text has been necessary, have not been transliterated into Latin alphabet with any uniformity. Early writers simply relied on their own ear and memory and made haphazard transliterations, the best they could. There was a natural tendency to adopt the existing sounds of the language in which the text was written. Early British writers often represented Persian words as if pronounced by Arabs or Indians; this was no doubt due to greater familiarity, through their Empire, with Arabic and Urdu.

What has complicated the issue further is the fact that, although an Indo-European tongue, Persian is written with the Arabic alphabet. This is a beautiful but cumbersome script, quite unsuited to Persian. A number of vowels are left out and there are duplicating letters for some of the consonants which in Arabic stand for slightly differing sounds, but are pronounced identically in Persian. In addition, there is the problem of Arabic words which have come into usage. Although these words are pronounced in a distinctly Persian way, and are subject to Persian syntax, the purists insist on their transliteration into Latin as if pronounced by Arabs. The use of the phonetic system, which has found a degree of frequency in more recent publications, in my view complicates the matter through the use of excessive diacritical marks, above and below the letters, signifying differences which are, at least for the Persian language, theoretical and not actual.

The system used in this book attempts to simplify the problem of transliteration and conveys as close a pronunciation to the Persian as possible. Admittedly Persian is subject to variations in many dialects within the country, as well as outside the present boundaries of Iran. My model is the pronunciation of the capital city, Tehran, which is by far the greatest urban centre of population in the Persian-speaking world.

In this system the doubling of letters has been avoided. There are seven distinct vowels in the Persian language, as represented by the following letters:

a	as in	apple
ā	as in	mark
e	as in	fence
i	as in	fierce
o	as in	hotel
ō	as in	role
u	as in	brute

The consonants in Persian are represented by the following letters:

b	as in	English
č	as in	chair
d	as in	English
f	as in	English
g	as in	give
h	as in	English
j	as in	English
k	as in	English
l	as in	English
m	as in	English
n	as in	English
p	as in	English
q	as in	a gutteral g similar to the German r
r	as in	English
s	as in	English
š	as in	shine
t	as in	English
v	as in	English
x	as in	a gutteral k similar to German ch as in Bach
y	as in	yellow (never as a vowel)
z	as in	English
ž	as in	measure

An apostrophe (') after a vowel (as in Ma'sum) or after a consonant (as in Mas'ud) results in a slight halt, at that point, in the flow of the sound.

Opening statement

The name Persia and the adjective Persian seem to have been practically expunged from common usage in the English language. Even the Persian Gulf has become The Gulf, as if there were no other gulfs on this planet. For the language spoken in Persia, the word Farsi is finding increasing currency. In the context of an English sentence one would not use the words Deutsch or Française for language spoken in Germany and France, but Farsi and not Persian is being used to designate the language of Persia.

A curious conspiracy seems to be at work to disinherit Iran and to distance her from her past, her glories, her ancient civilisation, and her considerable contributions to world culture, all of which are associated with the name Persia. As if Persia is no more; it has gone the way of Etruria, Babylon or Lydia. As if, now, there is only Iran, a new country, an artificially created political entity of the twentieth century, like so many others in the Middle East and Africa.

Of course, Iran is Persia and so it has always been. It is one of the very few ancient civilisations which has maintained its identity and individuality, with a marked degree of continuity, for more than twenty-five centuries. To be sure, properly speaking, Persia is only the south central region of Iran, but for sound historical reasons, from the sixth century BC to only a few years ago, the outside world has known all of Iran as Persia, and that is how it should have remained. Germany, Greece, Egypt, Finland, Japan and a number of other countries are known internationally by names different from the 'correct' native names. It would be confusing, and counter-productive to the interests of these countries, if they were to insist on the use of the native names by the outside world.

Unfortunately, misplaced notions of self-assertion led the Persian government, in the 1930s, to require the use of the native name Iran by foreign powers. In the post-World War II period, Persia has increasingly attracted international attention. Conflicts with the Soviet Union, oil crises, the reforms and excesses of the monarchy, and finally the revolution which has brought the clerics into power, have made daily headlines, all in the name of Iran. Correspondingly, Persia seems to have receded into an ever greater obscurity.

For my part, as ineffectual as it may be judged to be, I do not choose to contribute to this regrettable process of disassociating Iran with her past, and, as such, I have remained faithful to Persia. The adjective Persian is also what I have always used for all things pertaining to Persia, including her music.

Persian traditional music embodies two distinct types: the rural folk music and the urban art music. A country as vast as Persia (equal to the combined areas of Spain, France, the Low Countries, West Germany and Italy) necessarily possesses a folk music of great variety, particularly since her population (current estimates 50,000,000) includes diverse ethnic groups. No definitive study of Persian folk music has ever been made as the sheer scope of such a task makes it forbidding.

1

The urban art music, on the other hand, is a tradition within the domain of the memory of a limited number of musicians. It is represented by a body of pieces which have been transmitted by rote, from generation to generation, for many centuries. Each piece revolves around unspecified central nuclear melodies which the individual performer comes to know through experience and absorption. The manifestation of the skeletal melodic outlines into a piece of music varies greatly from one performance to another, depending on the degree of freedom assumed in extemporisation. Within certain modal restraints, the music is fluid, subjective and highly improvisatory. It is rhythmically, also generally, free and flexible. The wealth of this music, therefore, is not in complex rhythmic patterns, nor in polyphony, which it does not employ, but in the many modal possibilities and the cultivation of highly embellished melodies. It is a personal and illusive art of great subtlety and depth. It is a difficult art to study, to understand and to communicate.

In the pages that follow, I have attempted to unravel, discuss and explain this musical tradition with as much systematisation as it is possible to apply to an art which is so free of systems. The work is limited to the study of the contemporary tradition of the twelve *dastgāh*s, although brief chapters have been devoted, at the outset, to historical and theoretical matters. Chapters 4 through 15 cover each of the twelve *dastgāh*s, and each chapter is conceived on the following format:

1.   Analysis of the mode of the *dastgāh*.
2.   Discussion of the *forud* (cadential pattern) of the *dastgāh*.
3.   The *daramad* (opening pieces.)
4.   Discussion of the main *guše*s (pieces) within the *dastgāh*, including:
    a. Modulation to and from a *guše*;
    b. Analysis of the mode of the *guše*;
    c. Nuclear theme of the *guše*;
    d. Transcription of an improvisation on the nuclear theme.

Chapters 16 and 17 cover two categories of pieces which stand apart from the improvised body of pieces within each *dastgāh*, but are nonetheless important aspects of the tradition.

Scales and short musical examples are given in the text; longer musical examples are placed in the Appendix. All transcription and analyses were made from recordings of performances on *tār* and *setār* by different musicians, particularly those of my own teacher Nasrollāh Zarrinpange. He, in turn, had been a pupil of Musa Ma'rufi and Ma'rufi's *radif* was the basis of his teaching and performance.

1 A brief historical perspective

Of the musical arts of the earliest civilisations on the Iranian plateau, no tangible trace has remained. The Persian Empire of the Achaemenian dynasty (550–331 BC), with all its grandeur and glory, has left us nothing to reveal the nature of its musical culture. In the writings of the Greek historians, we find but a faint glimmer of the musical life of this period. Herodotus mentions the religious rituals of the Zoroastrians, which involved the chanting of sacred hymns. Xenophon, in his *Cyropedia*, speaks of the martial and ceremonial musics of the Persian Empire.[1]

The first document of any extent on Persian music comes to us from the Sassanian period (AD 226–642). At the Sassanian court, musicians had an exalted status. Emperor Chosroes II (Xosrō Parviz), ruler from AD 590 to 628, the splendour of whose court is told in many legends, was patron to numerous musicians. Rāmtin, Bāmšād, Nakisā, Āzād, Sarkaš and Bārbod were among the musicians of this period whose names have survived.

Bārbod was the most illustrious musician of the court of Chosroes II. Numerous stories about this musician and his remarkable skills as performer and composer have been told by later writers and poets. Bārbod is credited with the organisation of a musical system containing seven modal structures, known as the Royal Modes (*Xosrovāni*); thirty derivative modes (*Lahn*); and three hundred and sixty melodies (*Dastān*). The numbers correspond with the number of days in the week, month and year of the Sassanian calendar, but the implications are not clear.[2]

We do not know what these modes and melodies were, but a number of their names have been related by the writers of the Islamic era. These names suggest a remarkable diversity of musical types and expression. Such titles as 'Kin-e Iraj' (the Vengeance of Iraj), 'Kin-e Siāvuš' (the Vengeance of Siāvuš), and 'Taxt-e Ardešir' (the Throne of Ardešir) seem to refer to historic events, and must have been epic songs. 'Bāq-e Širin' (the Garden of Širin [The Queen]), 'Bāq-e Šahryār' (the Sovereign's Garden), and 'Haft Ganj' (the Seven Treasures) seem to have been concerned with the glories of the court of Chosroes. And still others, such as 'Sabz Bahār' (the Green Spring), 'Māh abar Kuhān' (Moon over the Mountains), and 'Rōšan Čerāq' (Bright Lights) must have been compositions of a descriptive nature. Unfortunately, one can do no more than speculate about the nature of these compositions; nothing is known about the theories on which they were based.

On the other hand, the musical documents from the ensuing Islamic period abound in references to the music of the Sassanian era. An investigation of these works leaves little doubt that the music of the Sassanian period had been the germinating seed from which much of the music of the Islamic civilisation grew.[3]

With the conquest of the Persian Empire by the Arabs (AD 642), for a period of nearly six centuries, Persia remained nominally within the framework of the vast Moslem Empire. In Persia, the Arabs found a culture considerably in advance of their own.[4] Very soon after the

3

conquest, Persian musicians were imported into every corner of the Moslem world. With the ascendancy of the Abbasid dynasty (A D 750–1258), the seat of the Caliphate was moved from Damascus to Baghdad, within former Persian territory. From this time on, Persian musicians and scholars in all fields became the dominant figures in the formation and development of Islamic culture.[5]

I should point out here that it has been customary to recognise the Persian scholars of the Abbasid period as Arabs. This error, which has been consistently perpetuated even by some of the most reputable of Western authors, is primarily due to two reasons: firstly, the Persians, at that time, usually wrote in Arabic, as that language was the *lingua franca* of the Empire and was the language of the patron princes. Secondly, the Persians also bore Arabic/Moslem names, although they frequently sustained surnames which identified their place of birth; e.g.: Abolfaraj Esfahāni, Safiaddin Ormavi, Ali Jorjani, etc. Most western writers have failed to associate these surnames with a place of birth.

It may be argued that the issue of national origins should not be emphasised, as the broad amalgamation of national and cultural traits brought about during the Abbasid period seems to have blurred the significance of such issues. On the other hand the credit which is given to the Arabs is not their due. If 'Islamic' were the sole identification perhaps major objections could be removed, provided that Islamic is not taken to be synonymous with Arabian. As the present study deals specifically with Persian music, however, the common error of misplacing some of the key progenitors of this culture should be rectified.

At the outset, Islamic religious leaders had assumed a hostile attitude towards music, and regarded it as a corrupting frivolity. But under the Abbasids, whose court was fashioned after that of the earlier Sassanian emperors, and whose rule had become increasingly more secular, music and musicians flourished. Of the musicians whose fame, and in some instances whose writings on music have survived, I shall mention a few, but shall forgo a detailed discussion of their lives and works:

1. **Ebrāhim Museli** (742–803): born of a Persian family in Kufa. Singer and *ud* (lute) player of the courts of Mahdi and Hārun al-Rashid, he is known to have composed more than nine hundred songs. He had studied music in Rey, Persia, with a Zoroastrian by the name of Javānaviye.
2. **Es'hāq Museli** (766–849): the son of Ebrāhim. Singer, composer and poet of great fame, author of a number of books on music, none of which has survived.
3. **Abu Nasr Fārābi** (872–950): the great musical theorist whose writings on scales, intervals, modes, rhythm and the construction of instruments became the basis for the writings of all Moslem theorists who followed him. He based his scientific investigations of music on the theories of the Classical Greeks, and was instrumental in reviving these early theories. His monumental book, *Ketab al-Musiqi al-Kabir*, has survived. He was from Fārāb, a town in the greater Khorāsān, and may indeed have been of a Turkic stock as is generally claimed.
4. **Abolfaraj Esfahāni** (896–966): music historian whose famous book, *Aqāni*, contains biographical accounts of the famous musicians of the early Abbasid period.
5. **Abu Ali Ebn-e Sinā (Avicenna)** (980–1037): illustrious philosopher, physician and musician who also based his studies on the theories of the Greeks, and expanded on the writings of Fārābi.
6. **Safiaddin Ormavi** (died 1294): also a theorist of great fame whose two books on musical theory, *Resāle al-Šarafiyye* and *Ketāb al-Advār*, contain numerous additions to the modal schemes given by Fārābi and Ebn-e Sinā. His definitive theory of intervals became the most

accepted basis for the recognition of modes throughout the Islamic Middle East. (See chapter 2).

7. **Qotbaddin Mahmud Širāzi** (1236–1312): author of an important musical encyclopedia which contains examinations of the theories of Fārābi and Safiaddin, as well as his original contributions, and a complex system of musical notation.
8. **Abdadqāder Marāqi** (died 1434): the last great theorist of the pre-modern era; author of several books on scales, modes and musical instruments, in one of which he had employed a system of musical notation.

From the sixteenth to the beginnings of the twentieth century musical scholarship seems to have suffered a decline in Persia. In these four centuries no work of any consequence was produced on music. This was the period of Shiite ascendancy. It is assumed that the proscriptive attitude of the Shiite clerics and their measure of dominance in the social affairs of the country may have been largely responsible for this musical stagnation.

It is true, however, that music as an art of performance was patronised by the imperial court and by the nobility both during the Safavid dynasty (1501–1722) and the Qajar dynasty (1785–1925). In fact, the emergence of the present system of twelve *dastgāh*s is primarily a development of the Qajar period. On the other hand, music was relegated more and more to a private endeavour existing under a cloud of suspicion.

From the beginnings of the twentieth century, influenced by growing westernisation, not only was musical performance elevated to a more publicly accessible position but musical scholarship was increasingly revived.

During the Pahlavi dynasty's rule (1925–1979), reforms towards the modernisation and westernisation of Persia received great momentum. By the mid-1930s, a *conservatoire* in Tehran with many European teachers was producing musicians and performers in the tradition of western art music. A symphony orchestra was formed and choral groups had been organised. Concerts of Persian traditional music, largely through the efforts of Ali Naqi Vaziri, were given.

The post-World War II period brought intense westernisation to Persia. By the 1970s the musical life of Tehran in particular was comparable to that in many large European cities. A very active opera company, a fine symphony orchestra, a ballet company, chamber groups, music festivals and concerts by visiting international artists and groups provided a crowded musical life for the capital. The radio and television network made available to the public throughout the country every variety of music, native and international, light and serious, to suit all palates. In addition to the *conservatoire* and the School of National Music, the University of Tehran had a large Music Department which trained students in western musicology and composition, as well as offering courses on Persian traditional music.

In addition to large numbers of highly placed performers (singers, pianists, violinists, conductors, etc.) and composers who were trained both within the country and through education abroad, a number of well-qualified musicologists have emerged. Ali Naqi Vaziri and Mehdi Barkešli will be discussed in chapter 2 of this book. Among other musicologists, the most prominent is Mohammad Taqi Mas'udiye who was educated in France and Germany and who has published books and articles on both Persian classical and folk music.

In recent years, a number of western scholars have taken an interest in Persian music and have produced books and articles of considerable importance. The eminent American musicologist Bruno Nettl has published two books and a number of articles representing his varied interests in Persian music. Ella Zonis carried out research in the 1960s and has produced a book of general interest. Stephen Blum has done penetrating studies on the folk music of certain regions and has published a number of important articles. Nelly Caron and Jean During are two French scholars who have done research on Persian music and have published a book each.

Since the revolution of 1978–9, and the renewed ascendancy of Shiite clerics, music has once more been placed in a position of disfavour. A certain amount of musical activity, mainly in the service of the state's ideological promotion, is being encouraged. All other activity is suppressed. The fate of music, both native and international, in Persia remains a matter of serious concern. Should the present regime remain in power and the current reactionary attitude be maintained, lasting damage to the musical culture of a venerable civilisation could be the inevitable outcome.

2 *Intervals and scales in contemporary Persian music*

In the course of the twentieth century, three separate theories on intervals and scales of Persian music have been proposed. The first of these, put forward in the 1920s by Ali Naqi Vaziri, identifies a 24-quarter-tone scale as the basis for Persian music. A second theory was formulated in the 1940s by Mehdi Barkešli according to which Persian music is defined within a 22-tone scale. The third view, arrived at by the present writer, isolates five intervals with which all modes are constructed and no longer recognises a 'basic scale' concept. In the following each of these three theories is explained and examined.

The 24-quarter-tone scale

The notion of the division of the scale into intervals of equal size has been the outcome of a western musical orientation. The fact that the European classical tradition, in its pursuit of a versatile technique of harmony, had developed the equal temperament, captured the imagination of those Middle Eastern musicians who came in contact with it. These musicians viewed the absence of harmony in their own music as a sign of its inferiority to western music. The desired musical advancement was thought possible only through the adoption of western harmonic practice. That, in turn, required equidistant tones.

There was a general awareness that the whole-tone and the semi-tone alone were not able to represent eastern music, which contained intervals unmistakably different from these two. In order to accommodate these 'irregular' intervals, a convenient solution seemed to lie in the adoption of the quarter-tone, and not the semi-tone, as the smallest unit.

The fact that such an arbitrary procedure of equalisation would distort the authenticity of their native music worried them little. To them, the ultimate goal was to rescue their music from its 'backward' state and to bring it to the advanced level of European music, which meant making possible the adoption of practical harmony. To achieve this goal any sacrifice was justifiable.

Already in the nineteenth century the Syrian musician, Mikhail Mashaqa, had proposed that the Turko-Arabian music could be best articulated in the context of a 24-quarter-tone scale.

In Persia, western musical influence began to be felt in the second half of the nineteenth century. Nāseraddin Shah, who ruled from 1848 to 1896, visited Europe on three different occasions. He and his entourage came in contact with western music mostly at state banquets and ceremonial occasions, when he was received by European monarchs and heads of state. He was quite impressed by the pomp of these ceremonies, to which military bands and orchestras had much to contribute. In the 1860s, after his first European tour, he ordered the establishment of a music school for the creation of an imperial military band. The school, organised and taught by French instructors, was mainly concerned with the teaching of wind instruments as well as the rudiments of western notation and theory.

Through this school's modest beginnings, Persia's first contacts with occidental music were made with the following consequences:

1.   Through the study of the rudiments of western musical theory, the concept of a fixed pitch, major and minor scales, keys, etc. were learnt, none of which had any application in the native music.

2.   Persian music was never submitted to any kind of notation. Isolated examples of notation found in medieval treatises were never an aspect of musical practice. They were tools of theoretical argumentation. Performing musicians had always learnt the music by rote and extemporised on the basis of modal and melodic models absorbed through experience. That is why composition was never developed into an art separate from performance. It was an aspect of performance and, as such, free from the need, or indeed the desirability, of being notated. In the school of music, students had to learn foreign music from notation so that they might be able to repeat it each time without alteration.

3.   There was no Persian band music in existence. Inevitably the music taught at the school was standard western pieces for military bands, such as marches, polkas, waltzes, airs and the like. By learning such pieces, students came to appreciate the major and minor modes and, more importantly, the clarity of melodic and rhythmic forms. By comparison, only Persian folk music possessed this sort of melodic simplicity and rhythmic directness; the classical tradition, on the other hand, is melodically very ornate and rhythmically free and non-committal.

4.   In studying the rudiments of harmony, students were impressed by the complete novelty of the use of more than one sound at the same time in a regulated and systematic way.

5.   For use in military bands, western musical instruments were imported and taught. These woodwind and brass instruments were essentially incapable of producing intervals peculiar to native music. Later, other instruments were brought into the country. The violin, in particular, found great favour among the local musicians as it could fully express the intervals and nuances of Persian music. Quite to the contrary is the case of the piano, also introduced in the late nineteenth century, as it is undoubtedly the most unsuitable of instruments for Persian music.

6.   Finally, the school of music introduced into Persia the idea of a methodical and pedagogically organised approach to the study of music. In the traditional way, the study of music was confined to the study of an instrument according to the personal methods of a teacher; any knowledge of the music itself was only incidental to the practical training. Western procedure introduced the idea of the uniformity of systematic study integrating the technique of performance with theoretical learning, all of which was written and taught with uniformity and precision.

Among the many pupils who received training at the school a few emerged as significant musical figures who became influential in setting the course of musical developments in the twentieth century. The most outstanding of these was Ali Naqi Vaziri (1886–1981), an energetic and highly intelligent man, who rapidly rose to the rank of colonel in the army. Vaziri was an excellent musician of the classical tradition and a virtuoso performer of the *tār* and the *setār*. However, he was fascinated by what he had learned of western music theory and, like many of his generation, was fired with zeal for westernisation.

Ali Naqi Vaziri was the first Persian to seek a musical education in Europe. He set out for France just before World War I and remained in Europe for some eight years. In France he studied harmony and composition and became familiar with a number of European instruments, such as the violin and the piano. In 1922 Vaziri produced the first of his several publications. The book, *Dastur-e Tār*, is ostensibly on the technique of the *tār* and contains exercises and pieces, from simple to difficult, for that instrument. The short text preceding the notated pieces, however, is far more important as it contains Vaziri's theory of Persian music. It is in this short introductory section of *Dastur-e Tār* that, for the first time, the view that Persian music relies on a 24-quarter-tone scale is expressed.

On his return to Persia in the early 1920s, Vaziri quickly became the most influential force in the country's musical life. He established a school of music of his own and set about training young musicians according to western methods. He remained faithful to Persian musical traditions but submitted those traditions to what he viewed as necessary reforms on the western model. His tireless activities, in addition to running the school and teaching, included writing books on methods of performance of *tār* (a second book) and the violin, giving public lectures, organising concerts, and in general promoting his new ideas on the reform of the national music. He wrote numerous compositions for solo instruments, particularly the *tār*, emphasising technical virtuosity, an aspect of music which the native art had never considered as an end in itself. He also wrote songs and even operettas. The most important of his books was *Musiqi-ye Nazari*, published in Tehran in 1934. In this book he elaborated on his theory of the 24-quarter-tone scale and gave an account of the twelve *dastgāh*s (five *dastgāh*s and seven *naqme*s, as he calls them), in a highly personal and selective way.

All through the twenties and the thirties Vaziri dominated the musical scene. He was 'the' educated musician who articulated theories and had western training. As traditional Persian musicians were reduced, for many generations, to virtually illiterate musicians who knew only how to perform and could not discuss their own music scientifically, the emergence of Vaziri as the one exception placed him in a position of unquestioned authority.

Vaziri's quarter-tone theory, which is arrived at by way of a further division of the western equidistant 12-note chromatic scale, is entirely irrelevant to Persian music. It is an artificial creation devised to make possible the adoption of a kind of harmonic practice, based on western tonal harmony. It would be difficult to accept that Vaziri was not aware of the fact that Persian music makes no use of the quarter-tone and that intervals other than the semi-tone and the whole-tone are not achieved through multiples of the quarter-tone. He must simply have believed in the desirability of their being adjusted to correspond to an equidistant quarter-tone scale so that a kind of harmony may be imposed upon the music. Clearly, he did not propose to do this in order to destroy the music, but, as he saw it, to advance its possibilities into the realm of polyphony. He and many other Middle Eastern musicians of the early twentieth century regarded a monophonic musical tradition as intrinsically inferior. Their aim was to make the necessary adjustments so that polyphonic writing could be admitted into their music, and understandably they took western music as their model.

Vaziri's pupils, and their pupils in turn, have remained totally committed to the ideas of the great master. Not only was he 'the' educated musician who 'knew what he was talking about', but he was also endowed with a charismatic and forceful personality which seems to have subjugated all who came in contact with him.

I met Ali Naqi Vaziri only once, in 1958. He was retired and in semi-seclusion at the time. I was taken to his home, in a mountain village in the suburb of Tehran, by his devoted disciple Ruhollah Xāleqi, who had become a close friend of mine during the period when I conducted my early research on Persian music. Vaziri was 72 at the time, and I found him to be far more vigorous and lucid than any other musician I had interviewed.

Although Vaziri's theoretical views must be unequivocally refuted, the importance of this musician in the twentieth-century developments of Persian music cannot be overestimated. He was a man of unquestionable integrity and his devotion to the 'cause' of Persian music, as he saw it, was boundless. His innovations in the notation of Persian music have become the standard and, in the present book, I have used the two signs *koron* (p) and *sori* (✳) which he invented to indicate the microtonal lowering and raising of tones, although, as used by him and his school, they are meant to lower and raise a pitch by an exact quarter-tone.

The 22-tone scale

More than any other contemporary figure, Mehdi Barkešli has endeavoured to find a scientifically accurate basis for the scale of Persian music. His findings are grounded in the theories of medieval writers, particularly those of Abu-Nasr Fārābi and Safiaddin Ormavi. Barkešli, a physicist by profession, made an extensive investigation, in the 1940s, into the measurement of the intervals of Persian music. Before evaluating his findings it is necessary to give a synopsis of the medieval theories of intervals upon which Barkešli's theories rest.

By the time of Fārābi (tenth century), the Pythagorean intervals of limma and comma had become the basis of the fretting of musical instruments. The octave contained two conjunct tetrachords and a whole tone. Each tetrachord yielded five pitches and four intervals. The five pitches were named after the open string and the four fingers which produced them when pressed on any of the strings of the *ud*. Taking the open string (*Motlaq*) as the pitch C, the pitches shown in figure 1 were produced by the stopping of the string.

Figure 1

Motlaq

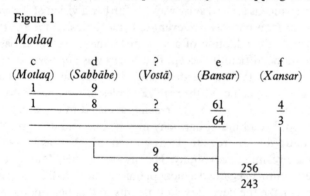

The positions of *Sabbābe* (index finger) and *Bansar* (ring finger) were clear and the intervals produced were a natural whole-tone and a major third from the *Motlaq*, respectively. The position of the *Vostā* (middle finger), however, became a subject of controversy.

The earliest known *Vostā* was achieved by descending a whole-tone from the *Xansar* (little finger) (f). This *Vostā* yields the Pythagorean minor third (e♭), which is higher than the *Sabbābe* (d) by an interval of $^{256}/_{243}$, the Pythagorean limma. This e♭, which I shall call v_1 produces the interval of $^{32}/_{37}$ from the *Motlaq* (c).

By Fārābi's time, four other positions for the *Vostā*, or four other possibilities of flattened e had been arrived at:

1. *Vostā-ye Fārs*, at a distance of $^{81}/_{68}$ from the *Motlaq* (v_2).
2. Old style *Vostā*, at a distance of $^{6}/_{5}$ from the *Motlaq* (v_3).
3. *Vostā-ye Zalzalāin*, at a distance of $^{19863}/_{16384}$ from the *Motlaq*. This is the same as the Pythagorean $d^{\sharp}$ (v_4).
4. *Vostā-ye Zalzāl*, at a distance of $^{27}/_{22}$ from the *Motlaq* (v_5).

Accordingly, the five possibilities of *Vostā*, in order of their distance from the *Motlaq*, in cents, are as shown in figure 2.

Figure 2

Motlaq	v_1	v_2	v_3	v_4	v_5
	294	303	315	320	354

The five *Vostās* provided five minor thirds from the open string, the last of which is too large and is roughly half-way between a minor and major third. This interval was called the neutral third of *Zalzāl*, named after the famous musician Mansur Ja'far Zalzāl who lived a century and a half before Fārābi and who favoured this particular *Vostā*.

In relation to the Sabbābe (d), the five *Vostās* provide five semi-tones. In order of their size, in cents, the five semi-tones are as shown in figure 3.

Figure 3

Sabbābe	v_1	v_2	v_3	v_4	v_5
	90	99	111	116	150

From these five *Vostās* to *Xansar* (f), we arrive at the intervals shown in figure 4.

Figure 4

v_1	v_2	v_3	v_4	v_5	*Xansar*
204	195	183	178	144	

In the medieval scale, another variable tone was located between the *Motlaq* and the *Sabbābe*; it was called the *Zāed*. According to various systems and theories, five *Zāeds* or five $d^{\flat}$s were known. In relation to the *Motlaq*, these five *Zāeds* represent the ratios of: $^{256}/_{243}$,

$^{18}/_{17}$, $^{2187}/_{2048}$, $^{162}/_{140}$, and $^{54}/_{49}$. I shall refer to these five *Zāeds* as z_1, z_2, z_3, z_4 and z_5 respectively. The measurement of these intervals in cents is shown in figure 5. The first of

Figure 5

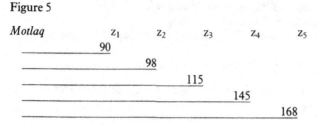

these is equal to the Pythagorean limma; the second is nearly equal to the tempered semi-tone; the third is appreciably larger than the semi-tone; the last two are roughly in between the semi-tone and the whole-tone.

There is not much point in showing the measurement between *Vostā* and *Bansar* or *Zāed* and *Sabbābe*; these intervals had no practical application. In other words, if a *Vostā* or a variety of e^b was employed, it was to replace the *Bansar* (e), and the chromatic progression from e^b to $e^{\natural}$ was not used. Similarly, d^b to $d^{\natural}$ was a chromatic interval which, while theoretically possible, was avoided in practice. In fact, the various *Zāeds* in themselves had a limited usage, mostly as ornamental tones.

Evidently, different musicians showed preference for one or more of the five *Vostās* and the five *Zāeds*. For example, the tetrachord attributed to Es'hāq Museli contains only v_1 and no *Zāed*. The tetrachord of Ya'qub al-Kindi contains v_1 and z_1; in Fārābi's tetrachords v_1, v_2 and v_5 and z_1, z_2, z_4, z_5 are used.

Ebn-e Sinā (Avicenna), the illustrious successor to Fārābi, added a new *Vostā* and two new *Zāeds* to the already large possibilities. The new *Vostā* (v_6) represents an interval of $^{39}/_{32}$, or 343 cents from the *Motlaq*. The two *Zāeds* (z_6 and z_7) represent intervals of $^{16}/_{15}$ and $^{13}/_{12}$, or 111 and 139 cents from the *Motlaq* respectively.

In the thirteenth century, Safiaddin Ormavi set out to remedy the confusion of the *Vostā* and the *Zāed*. He ruled out all except v_1 and z_1 from his tetrachord. He added, however, a new *Vostā* (v_7) and a new *Zāed* (z_8). He arrived at these new intervals by finding a pitch at a perfect fifth above z_1; a whole-tone below this pitch (x) will give the v_7 and a whole-tone below v_7 gives the z_8 of Safiaddin. In admitting these two intervals, plus v_1 and z_1, into the structure of the tetrachord the following division of the tetrachord is arrived at:

Motlaq	z_1	z_8	Sabbābe	v_1	v_7	Bansar	Xansar
Limma	Limma	Comma		Limma	Limma	Comma	Limma
90c	90c	24		90	90	24	90

The division of this tetrachord was duplicated in a succeeding conjunct tetrachord. The remaining whole-tone, to complete the octave, was also divided into two limmas and a comma. The scale of Ormavi, therefore, has the following succession of intervals:

$$L, L, C - L, L, C - L + L, L, C - L, L, C - L + L, L, C$$

This neatly organised 17-tone scale became the universally accepted basis for the theory of music throughout the Islamic world for many centuries. It must be understood, however, that such an exact scale system may have been, in practice, highly flexible. This was the scale of the theoreticians, and we have only their account of the musical system and of modes. To what extent music, in its actual practice, supported such exactitude is open to debate. It is my belief that musical performance must have been far more fluid and variable. There were no instruments of fixed pitch in use and vocal music is notoriously unreliable as to the maintenance of any scale division requiring great precision. The considerable flexibility of intervals in today's music cannot be a new development. It is quite reasonable to assume that comparable variability was in evidence in medieval times.

The 17-tone scale does not contain the interval of a quarter-tone or anything approximating it. The comma, which is close to an eighth of a tone, was never used by itself; it was merely added to or taken from a larger interval. It is also important to stress that no piece of music and no mode has ever made use of all the seventeen tones. The music was conceived within modes containing a limited number of pitches from the available seventeen tones. The majority of modes were heptatonic, a few had less or more than seven tones in the octave. The 17-tone scale was only as meaningful to the practice of music as the 12-tone chromatic scale would be to the music of the Middle Ages and the Renaissance. It would be therefore misleading to overemphasise the significance of this scale in so far as the practical art of music was concerned.

After several centuries when no theoretical research was undertaken, in the 1940s, Mehdi Barkešli conducted a series of tests, using various kinds of apparatus, to determine the size of Persian intervals. Curiously enough, he made his measurements of intervals from recordings of vocal music. He had five reputable traditional musicians who sang pieces in various modes which he recorded and analysed.

From such analysis, Barkešli concluded that the whole-tone and the semi-tone in Persian music are stable and closely duplicate the same intervals in the Pythagorean classification. The major tetrachord of c, d, e, f gave the following intervals in cents: $206 + 204 + 89 = 499$, which is practically the same as the Pythagorean major tetrachord. The major seconds of 206 or 204 approximate the interval of two limmas and a comma, and the 89-cents interval is equal to a limma.

In other tetrachords, Barkešli found three variants of d^b and of e^b. The three d^b's, in relation to c produced these intervals in cents: 89 (d^b_1), 120 (d^b_2) and 181 (d^b_3). The three e^b's, in relation to d produced the exact same intervals: 89 (e^b_1), 120 (e^b_2) and 181 (e^b_3). Of these three intervals, the first (89 cents) is equal to a limma, also found in the major tetrachord (e to f). Barkešli identifies the 120-cents interval as the characteristic interval of Persian music but he states that the 181-cents interval has only rare usage.

Barkešli, who is very interested in linking his own findings with the scale of Ormavi, establishes that the d^b_1 (89 cents) is almost identical with the z_1, and the d^b_3 (181 cents) is practically the same as the z_8 of Ormavi's 17-tone scale. Similarly, the e^b_1 and e^b_3 of Barkešli parallel the v_1 and the v_7, respectively. But his d^b_2 and e^b_2, which he regards as the most characteristic intervals of Persian music, have no counterparts in the 17-tone scale.

As a consequence of his findings Barkešli concludes that the whole-tone in the contemporary tradition is not divided into $L + L + C$, but is divisible into L; $L + C$; $L + L$ and $L + L + C$ (see figure 6). According to this theory there are twenty-two tones to the octave as each whole-tone is divisible into four and there are five whole-tones plus two semi-tones in the octave. The interval that Barkešli has added to the intervals of the 17-tone scale is the $L + C$.

Figure 6

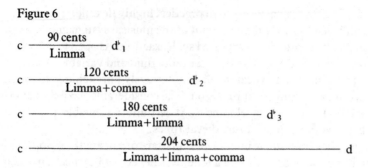

He equates this interval with the 120 cents d^b_2 and e^b_2; although in reality L + C is equal to 114 cents. In fact, the 17-tone scale of Ormavi, also, provides for the L + C interval. In his tetrachords, both z_1 to *Sabbābe*, and v_1 to *Bansar* are 114 cents.

Barkešli's most serious flaw in determining the intervals of Persian music is his commitment to the premise of the octave-scale and the fact that he measures intervals against imaginary points of reference. In so doing he takes an octave containing five whole-tones and two semi-tones as a point of departure. The pitches he has found are fitted into this seemingly inevitable container. As such he uses the same container as did Safiaddin and other medieval theoreticians. We cannot evaluate the validity of this approach by those classical scholars, but its irrelevance to the musical practices of today can be established.

The false container has seven tones arranged as in the scale of the Mixolydian mode, e.g., c-d-e-f-g-a-b^b-c. The intervals established by this scale are taken as basic fixtures; other pitches have been fitted among them. The result has been the 22-tone scale. In fact the 7-tone basic scale as a point of reference is arbitrary and misleading.

The very idea of the division of the whole-tone seems erroneous. The whole-tone is no more basic or legitimate than other intervals. The smaller intervals are not consequences of the division of the whole-tone; they exist for themselves.

The fallacy of the 'division of the whole-tone' can be illustrated by the fact that in so doing both of the two tones which produce this interval must be accounted for. That is to say, in considering the division of the interval between c and d both pitches must exist. In actual practice, however, if a flattened version of d is used it replaces that d natural. In no mode of Persian music do we find a kind of d^b followed by a d$^{\natural}$. One must conclude, therefore, that it is incorrect to consider the interval produced by d^b as a subdivision of c to d, since d does not exist. The same holds true in respect of the interval from d to e. If a version of e^b is used, then e$^{\natural}$ is invariably absent.

In the context of Persian modes, a d^b is always followed by either an e^b or e^p (slightly flat). Similarly an e^b is followed by f or f$^{\sharp\natural}$ (slightly sharp).

The whole confusion arises from the fact that, in accordance with western musical theory, flat or sharp notes are seen as altered versions of a natural tone. It would be far more satisfactory to have a separate identification for each pitch, as was done in medieval Islamic tradition and is still used in Turkish classical music. If each of the twelve, seventeen, twenty-two or twenty-four pitches had its own name, or letter identification, then one tone would not have been regarded as the raised or lowered version of another and the notion of the division of the whole-tone would not have arisen.

Whereas Vaziri's theories about Persian music found general acceptance and are still widely held, those of Mehdi Barkešli have made no impact at all. Vaziri's views, personal and arbitrary as they are, were put forth by a performing musician and a teacher of high standing. Furthermore, they were expounded at a time when no particular musical theory had currency and musicians had generally no competence to question them. Barkešli's findings, although resting on a certain amount of scientific research, were published in a French journal, and, as he was not a practising musician but a physicist, his theories did not attract the attention of the musical circles.

Both theories suffer equally from a tendency to accommodate certain western concepts. Each theory, by suggesting very exact intervals, remains oblivious to the fluidity and flexibility of Persian intervals. Vaziri did not take account of this instability, as his apparent objective was to make Persian music adhere to a process of equal temperament so that it can be harmonised. Barkešli, on the other hand, was not interested in the westernisation of Persian music but was committed to prove that today's music is still rooted in the medieval system. He has taken the exactness of the medieval theory very seriously – as have many others – and has proposed a system vested with even greater precision.

The theory of flexible intervals

My study of Persian music has brought me to certain conclusions distinctly different from those of other theorists. I am rather sceptical about the implications of medieval theories for the musical performance of the time. These theories were written by eminent scholars who, in most cases, were not practising musicians. They were philosophers, scientists and encyclopaedists who often wrote on every field of human knowledge including music. I tend to regard the precision inherent in these musical systems with some uncertainty. My doubts find some justification in the fact that today's musical traditions do not support the exactitude of those theories. Moreover, no Middle Eastern musical instrument is capable of producing intervals of such precision; and vocal music is even more unreliable in producing accurate intervals.

I find it particularly strange that Barkešli made his measurement of intervals from recorded vocal music. At least some musical instruments used in Persia are fretted; the frets are movable, but they still provide a higher degree of stability than singers do. Persian singers do not rely on any concept of a fixed pitch: they sing, as a rule, with some instrumental accompaniment. If there is any pitch discrepancy between the singer and the accompanist, it is the singer who makes the adjustment. The instrumentalist cannot revise the fretting of his instrument and he can only play a given mode in two or three different 'keys'.

For the measurement of intervals I used two *tār*s and three *setār*s which were fretted by reputable musicians. All five were instruments in actual use by native musicians and fretted to produce Persian music considered as authentic and accurate. Moreover, I made measurements of intervals from a large body of recorded music as played by well-known musicians. For the measurement I used a stroboconn and a melograph.

The result of these measurements showed that the whole-tone and the semi-tone are relatively stable. The whole-tone is slightly larger than the tempered whole-tone, approximating the interval of L + L + C (204 cents); the semi-tone is significantly smaller than the tempered one and is never larger than a limma (90 cents), often even slightly smaller.

Intervals that are larger than the semi-tone but smaller than the whole-tone, called neutral tones, are very flexible. Two separate neutral intervals can, however, be identified. A smaller neutral tone can fluctuate between 125 and 145 cents, the mean for which can be taken as 135 cents. A larger neutral tone fluctuates between 150 and 170 cents, the mean being 160 cents. In most cases these two intervals follow one another to complete a minor third.

Another interval, also very unstable, is larger than the whole-tone but not as large as the augmented tone. The mean size of this interval is 270 cents. In authentic Persian music the augmented tone is not used. The interval of approximately 270 cents is the least common of the basic intervals and is used in only a few of the modes. As there is no traditional name for this interval, and because I do not wish to confuse it with the augmented tone, I have called it the 'plus tone'. In the modes where this interval is used, it is always preceded by the small neutral tone; together they complete a major third.

On the basis of the foregoing, my classification of Persian intervals, with which various modes are created, is as follows:

1.   Semi-tone or minor 2nd (m) *ca.* 90 cents.
2.   Small neutral tone (n) *ca.* 135 cents.
3.   Large neutral tone (N) *ca.* 160 cents.
4.   Whole-tone or major 2nd (M) *ca.* 204 cents.
5.   Plus-tone (P) *ca.* 270 cents.

I do not believe that beyond the recognition of these intervals, and the possibility in their combinations, there is any concept of a 'scale' system governing Persian music today. Any notion of a particular 'scale' from which Persian modes are constructed is totally irrelevant. To be sure, such a notion is irrelevant to all musical traditions. The reality is the converse; that is, scales are artificial patterns of ascending or descending tones, within the range of an octave, derived from different musical practices. However, in some cultures such as the western classical and the Indian classical traditions, scales have in turn been utilised in creative and performance procedures and, as such, have become both relevant and important. In certain cultures this has not occurred and any emphasis on the notion of a 'basic scale', whether for the music as a whole or even for individual modes, can be misleading.

Persian musical terminology does not recognise the 'scale' and there is no word for it. The French word *gamme* has been adopted in recent times. Its usage has tended inadvertently to impose a frame of reference alien to the music. Still, today the majority of Persian performing musicians have no knowledge of what a scale is. They do not understand, should they be asked to play the scale of this or that mode. They see no point in playing the notes used in a mode as a descending or ascending scale. The musical context does not provide for such an exercise; it is therefore artificial and irrelevant.

Most Persian modes, in their elemental forms, can be expressed within a tetrachord or a pentachord. In some cases as many as seven or more tones are needed to convey the mode adequately. The octave is not significant. In certain modes a range of pitches beyond the limits of an octave is needed, as in the higher octave some notes are different from what they are in the lower octave.

At this point, it may be useful to examine the fretting system of those two instruments in the classical tradition which are fretted: *tār* and *setār*. They have an identical range, from C or D to about g' (see figure 7). Taking the main melody string with c as its open pitch, we find seventeen tones within the octave (see figure 8). It is curious that this octave contains

Figure 7

Figure 8

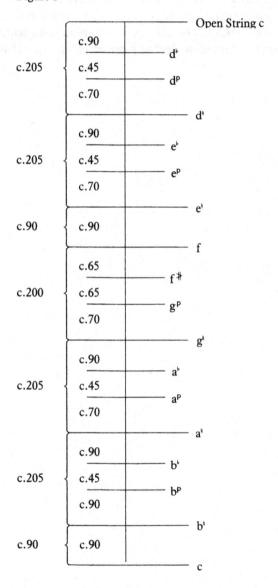

seventeen tones; however, they do not correspond to the seventeen tones of Safiaddin's scale. It would be impossible to establish whether this scale represents a distorted version of the Safiaddin scale, or whether his scale might be an idealised representation of something which might have been closer to the above. Some seven centuries have passed and the musical practices have been perpetuated through an aural tradition.

It must also be understood that the fretting system shown here has been provided to accommodate all the Persian modes within the given range. Any one mode does not require more than seven or eight pitches. Indeed, some modes may be adequately expressed within the range of a tetrachord or a pentachord. No chromaticism is used, e.g., e♭ and e♮, or f♯ and g♭ are not used in succession. Accordingly a 45-cents or a 70-cents interval, as shown in the above fretting, have no consecutive application in any one of the modes. No interval smaller than a semi-tone (*ca.* ninety cents) is ever used. The only exception is an ornamental trill from, for example, e♭ to e♭ which is used in certain modes but is not essential to the structure of those modes.

3   *Musical concepts and terminology*

This book is mainly concerned with an investigation of the complexities of the *dastgāh* system and the analysis of the structure of each of the twelve *dastgāh*s. It is useful, however, to establish an understanding, at the outset, as to what is meant by a *dastgāh*. Also, in this chapter, other terms and concepts peculiar to Persian music are explained so that reference to them can be made henceforth without the need for scattered explanations and footnotes.

Dastgāh (organisation, system)

A *dastgāh* has been taken to be the counterpart of the Indian *raga* and the *maqām* of the Turko-Arabian musical traditions. It has also been translated as a mode in western musical terminology. None of these describes a *dastgāh* adequately.

Two separate ideas are, in fact, addressed by the *dastgāh* concept. It identifies a set of pieces, traditionally grouped together, most of which have their own individual modes. It also stands for the modal identity of the initial piece in the group. This mode has a position of dominance as it is brought back frequently, throughout the performance of the group of pieces, in the guise of cadential melodic patterns.

Accordingly, a *dastgāh* signifies both the title of a grouping of modes, of which there are twelve, and the initial mode presented in each group. When we say, for example, *dastgāh-e Homāyun*, we mean a group of pieces under the collective name *Homāyun*; as a mode, however, *Homāyun* only identifies the initial piece of that collection. It would be wrong, therefore, to conclude that there are only twelve modes in Persian music; there are twelve groupings of modes, the totality of which represents some sixty modes. Each mode has its own proper name, but the opening section of the *dastgāh* has no specific name and is called *darāmad* (entry, introduction). The proper name of this opening section is that of the *dastgāh* itself.

The practice of grouping pieces into collections and the application of the term *dastgāh* is of a relatively recent origin. There is no evidence for the practice having existed prior to the Qājār period (1787–1925). For all we know, before the nineteenth century, modes or *maqām*s were performed individually, as they still are in the Turko-Arabian traditions. Presumably a series of improvisations and compositions were performed in the same mode to cover the desired length of time.

There is no clear information as to the reason why this practice was gradually abandoned in favour of the present system of stringing together different modes in a *dastgāh*. By way of conjecture, I tend to look for the reason in the general decline of musical scholarship in Persia, from the sixteenth to the twentieth century. I believe that the musicians' diminishing ability to compose and to extemporise within one mode to a desired length of time might have been responsible for the development of the present practice. To move from one mode to one or more other modes, in time, had become a convenient way of filling the desired period of a performance.

In all cultures the question of an acceptable length of a performance is of considerable importance. Even in modern times, when people's patience is more easily taxed, a performance lasting only a few minutes is not regarded as respectable. In former days, a musician was expected to play for a reasonably long period, and it was not acceptable to play a series of short and unrelated pieces. To cope with the expected time requirements, a musician had to produce lengthy and varied improvisations, and he was also expected to include a number of set compositions, all in the same mode. In all probability, as Persian musicians' performance ability and knowledge of musical literature declined, the practice of moving through a series of modes was adopted; by so doing, musicians were able to meet the time requirements. At the same time, to accommodate the necessary cohesion in the totality of a performance with no pauses, references to the opening mode were repeatedly made by way of the cadential formulae (*forud*).

In the Arabian and Turkish classical traditions, which have strong historic ties with that of Persia, the same problem brought about a different solution. Particularly in Turkey, from the seventeenth century, a strong tradition of group playing and group singing was developed. The sheer number and variety of forces provided greater possibilities in the presentation of each mode. In addition, the Ottomans produced a remarkable school of musical composition. Extemporised performance was enhanced by the growing number of well-defined composed pieces, whose addition to the repertoire of each mode made a long rendition of that mode easily attainable.

None of these developments took place in Persia until late in the nineteenth century. A lengthy presentation of Persian music had to be achieved either by way of sustained improvisations in one mode, or through stringing together a number of modes. Clearly, the latter was more feasible and also, probably, more interesting.

During the past one hundred years, the composition of clearly defined pieces and ensemble playing have come to play an increasingly important role in Persian music. At the same time, modern expectations place a lesser burden of length upon the performer. As a result the lengthy *dastgāh*s of the nineteenth century, with many modes woven into a whole tapestry, have been submitted to a steady trimming process. The normal performance duration of a *dastgāh* in modern times rarely exceeds thirty minutes. The thirty-minute time limit is, to some extent, imposed by allocated time for radio and television programmes. About half of this period is likely to be taken up by composed pieces; the improvised portions centre on the opening mode (*darāmad*) and two or three of the other modes in the *dastgāh*. Should musicians continue the process of reducing the group of pieces in a *dastgāh* to a mere few, and of adding composed pieces, an eventual return to the practice of performing in only one mode may result.

A further clarification of the *dastgāh* concept is required here. The prevailing notion among Persian musicians assigns the title *dastgāh* to only seven of the modal systems: *Šur*, *Segāh*, *Čahārgāh*, *Homāyun*, *Navā* and *Rāst-Panjgāh*. Four of the remaining five, *Abuatā*, *Bayāt-e Tork* (or *Bayāt-e Zand*), *Dašti* and *Afšāri* are classified as derivatives of *Šur*; the remaining, *Bayāt-e Esfahān* is considered to be a derivative of *Homāyun*. These five are not called *dastgāh*, but the word *āvāz* (song) is used as their generic title.

I have preferred to classify all twelve as *dastgāh*s. In so doing I am not defying a weighty or a long-standing tradition. It must be borne in mind that the whole system of the twelve groupings is not very old, and the classifications are fairly arbitrary and without strong reasoning. Ali Naqi Vaziri, some sixty-five years ago, challenged the common tradition and recognised only five *dastgāh*s. He believed that *Navā* is also a derivative of *Šur*, and he identified *Rāst-Panjgāh* with *Māhur*. Furthermore, he disliked the term *āvāz* and used the word *naqme* (note or melody) for 'derivative *dastgāh*s'.

The reason for recognising five, or seven, of the twelve as being derivative is that tradition, or Vaziri as the case may be, has viewed the five, or the seven, as less distinct in their initial modes than the others. The view has been that the dominant mode of a *dastgāh* must have very striking characteristics, including a very distinct structure of intervals. If the initial modes in two *dastgāh*s make use of the same pitch material, even when their functions and melodic dictates are different, then one of the modes is considered a dependant of the other. For example, it is said that if we begin and build from the fourth degree of the mode of *Homāyun*, we shall obtain *Bayāt-e Esfahān*. For that reason *Bayāt-e Esfahān* is known as a derivative of *Homāyun*. This is clearly a fallacious argument. If this were a valid basis for classification then western music would have but one mode; Phrygian could be regarded as a derivative of Dorian, as it begins on the second degree of that mode; Lydian begins on its third degree, Mixolydian on its fourth degree, etc.

The prevailing opinions, as well as those of Vaziri and others, have misunderstood what a mode is. A mode is not a mere assortment of pitches and the resultant intervals. Far more important is the function of the tones in the creation of music. Notes by themselves do not constitute music; it is in how they are put together that music is made.

In all modal concepts, and certainly in a musical tradition such as the Persian, where improvisation on the basis of certain melodic patterns is fundamental to musical creativity, functions of tones are of paramount importance. Any similarity in the pitch material of the modes of, say, *Homāyun* and *Bayāt-e Esfahān* is of little significance. What is important is whether or not the melodic patterns that form the frame of reference in both modes are the same. They certainly are not; had they been the same they would not have been identified with two different titles. I have therefore applied the term *dastgāh* equally to all the twelve groupings, some of which are more extensive than others in the number of pieces (*guše*s) which they include.

Radif (row, series)

The pieces that constitute the repertoire of Persian traditional music are collectively called the *radif*. To be sure, these are not clearly defined pieces but melody models upon which extemporisation takes place. The same piece never sounds quite the same twice, even as performed by the same person on the same day. It varies in content and in length, but certain elemental melodic features remain which give the piece its identity. In practice, the fundamental ingredient is not extracted, not even for teaching purposes. What I call the melody model is absorbed by the performing musician, as well as the informed listener, through repeated experience of hearing different renditions of the piece, over a long period of time.

The word *radif* is also used to denote the group of pieces that form each of the twelve *dastgāh*s. The *radif* of, for example, *Šur* indicates all the pieces (*darāmad*s, *guše*s and *tekke*s) which are within the organisation of *dastgāh-e Šur*.

Guše (corner, section, piece)

The generic term for individual pieces, other than the *darāmad*, which make up the repertoire of a *dastgāh*, is *guše*. As the length and importance of *guše*s vary greatly, and as there is no nomenclature to separate the important ones from fragmentary pieces frequently omitted in a performance, in this book I shall apply the term *tekke* to the latter. Pieces in the category of *tekke*, many of which can occur in more than one *dastgāh*, are treated in a separate chapter (chapter 16).

Darāmad (opening, introduction)

The piece, or the group of pieces in a common mode, which begin a *dastgāh* are called *darāmad*. They are the most representative portion of the *dastgāh*. The mode and the melodic patterns of the *darāmad* are those of the *dastgāh* itself. The *guše*s and the *tekke*s which follow present their own separate modes and their own individual titles. Therefore, the identity of the *dastgāh* is primarily established by the *darāmad* section.

Pišdarāmad (pre-introduction, overture)

A composed rhythmic instrumental piece which is sometimes performed at the beginning of a *dastgāh* is called a *pišdarāmad*. It is a twentieth-century innovation intended for ensemble playing. An increasing number of *pišdarāmad*s have been composed during the last eighty years (see chapter 17).

Čahārmezrāb (four plectra, four strokes)

This is a solo instrumental piece in the style of a study, in a fast tempo and in simple or compound duple metres. There is a limited number of *čahārmezrāb*s composed by the nineteenth-century masters. In the twentieth century, a large body of *čahārmezrāb*s has been composed as the form has become increasingly popular. At present, there is a tendency to include more than one *čahārmezrāb* in the performance of a *dastgāh*, as the virtuoso demands of such pieces serve to display the instrumentalist's technical prowess (see chapter 17).

Zarbi (rhythmic)

An improvisatory passage or short piece, instrumental or vocal, which is not in the usual free metre, but adheres to a fixed rhythmic pattern, regulated by duple, triple or quadruple metric structures, is called a *zarbi*. Rhythmic *tekke*s are in this category (see chapter 16).

Reng (dance)

A *reng* is an instrumental piece in duple or triple metre in a moderately fast tempo. It is intended as a dance piece but does not necessitate dancing. There are a few traditional *reng*s dating back to the nineteenth century or possibly before. There is a large body of twentieth-century *reng*s, composed by known composers. A striking similarity exists between the form of the *reng* and the *pišdarāmad*: whereas the former is an opening instrumental piece, the latter is an instrumental piece with which the performance of a *dastgāh* is usually concluded (see chapter 17).

Tasnif (ballad)

A composed song in a slow metre is called a *tasnif*. As is true of other forms of musical composition, most *tasnif*s are of relatively recent origin and by known composers.

A large number of *tasnif*s were composed during the first two decades of the twentieth century. Many of them are based on patriotic themes reflecting the spirit of the constitutional movement of that period. *Tasnif*s composed during the twenties and the thirties are more concerned with amorous topics and the poetry used is generally from the works of classical poets. In the post-World War II period, the poetic context has gradually become light and the music of the *tasnif* has been affected by western popular songs. This more 'modern' type of *tasnif* is generally called '*tarāne*' (see chapter 17).

Gām (scale)

I have made clear, in the previous chapter, that the concept of a musical scale is unknown to the practical art of Persian music. Playing or singing a scale, unless in a deliberate imitation of western music, is not practised by a traditional Persian musician. The musical terminology does not contain a word for a musical scale. However, with the prevalence of western musical theory, the French word *gamme* (gām) has been adopted.

In this book, as the theory of Persian music is necessarily explained with reference to western theory and for western readers, I have formulated scales for each of the modes under discussion. I have refrained from taking the octave as the necessary limit of these scales and have only represented the pitches needed to express each mode. Their arrangements, in an ascending order, may cover a range short of an octave, or, in some cases, longer than an octave, as some pitches in their higher octave do not remain the same as in the lower.

The finalis is not necessarily placed at the bottom of the scale; it is placed where it occurs in an actual nuclear melody. In keeping with this approach, I do not refer to this or that degree of the scale, but discuss various pitches in relation to the finalis, e.g. 3rd above, 4th below, etc.

Maqām (mode)

Before the development of the system of the twelve *dastgāhs*, traditional music was known under the genus of various *maqām*s. In Turkey and in the Arabic-speaking countries, the *maqāmāt* (arabic plural for *maqām*) is still the basis of classical music. In those countries, as well as in Persia before the development of the *dastgāh* system, *maqām* signified a mode, with its usual properties of pitch functions and intervals, plus a particular melodic format upon which improvisation and composition are created.

In Persian music, more analogous to *maqām* is *māye*, a word with increasing usage signifying precisely what is meant by a *maqām* elsewhere. However, it must be added that the word *maqām* has not been dropped altogether from the musical vocabulary. In fact, even the word 'mode' has come to be used. All three, *māye*, *maqām* and mode, can be and are used with identical implications.

Finalis

I have used the word finalis in preference to tonic which has direct associations with the harmonic system of western music. The finalis indicates the note of repose and conclusion and is abbreviated by the letter 'F'.

Āqāz (beginning)

The tone on which an improvisation in a mode usually begins is called the *āqāz* (abbreviated as 'Ā').

Ist (stop)

In some modes a tone other than the finalis serves as the ending note for phrases and in situations other than the final cadences. This tone is called the *ist* (abbreviated as 'I').

Šāhed (witness)

In most of the Persian modes one tone assumes a conspicuously prominent role. It may or may not be the finalis. It is called the *šāhed* (abbreviated as 'Š'). The term dominant should not be used, as that word has harmonic implications; furthermore, the *šāhed* is not necessarily the 5th degree of the scale.

Moteqayyer (changeable)

In some of the Persian modes one of the tones appears consistently in two different forms, e.g. E natural and E slightly-flat. When there is such a regularly fluctuating tone, it is called a *moteqayyer* (abbreviated as 'M').

It must be added here that in some modes the 3rd below the finalis, when leading to the 2nd below and then to the finalis, is raised by a microtone. As this is a peculiarity of cadential patterns and does not create a genuinely fluctuating tone, it is not considered as a *moteqayyer* but shall be referred to simply as the raised 3rd below.

Certain tones in Persian modes are lowered in the high octave. This is a peculiarity of tone register, not of mode. In vocal music, when most of the singing is well within a one octave range, towards the end of the improvisation, for a display of virtuosity, the singer may go beyond an octave, in which case the octave of the 2nd degree or the 3rd degree above the finalis may be lowered by a microtone or a semi-tone. For example, if the primary tetrachord of the mode has been a major tetrachord it may be changed to a minor tetrachord. This change will take place in descending movements only (e.g. f, e, d, c, is changed to f, e♭, d, c). In instrumental music, where ordinarily a range of two octaves and a 5th is available, the middle octave is the centre of melodic activity. As in vocal music, the melodic line in climactic sections is extended above this octave, and again the same type of lowering of pitches as mentioned above may take place. The definition of *moteqayyer* does not encompass this type of change in pitch, which is not an essential character of any mode, but shows an intuitive desire to achieve greater tension more tenable in the higher register of sound. It seems quite clear that this type of pitch lowering is an artifice not basic to the mode itself.

Forud (descent, cadence)

Forud is a melodic cadence with a relatively fixed pattern which is subject to variation through improvisation. In a *dastgāh* the role of the *forud* (of which there may be more than one type) is extremely important. It is the *forud* which binds together all of the various *tekke*s and *guše*s which are performed in that *dastgāh*. Most of these pieces are modally independent, but their conclusion with a familiar *forud* shows their dependence on the original mode introduced in the *darāmad* section of the *dastgāh*. We see, therefore, that the *forud*s are sometimes the sole agent for the unification of the group of pieces placed together under the heading of one *dastgāh*. As such, they justify the application of the title of the *dastgāh* to the whole group, even though many of the pieces in the group have nothing in common with the others or with the *dastgāh* proper as represented by the *darāmad*.

The length of a *forud* may vary considerably according to the whim of the performer. It can be condensed into a few notes or expanded into what may seem like a complete piece. Different possibilities in *forud*s will be demonstrated as individual *dastgāh*s are taken up.

Ōj (soar, height)

The traditional procedure for the succession of *guše*s in a *dastgāh* requires a gradual move from a relatively low sound register to a higher range. Consequently, the *darāmad* is usually performed in the bottom register of the voice or the instrument. The succeeding *guše*s are arranged in such a sequence as to bring about a gradual rise in pitch material. Usually the last few *guše*s are the highest in tonal range and they represent the *ōj* or the high point of a *dastgāh*.

The gradual flight from low to high, however, is far from being rigidly observed. Evidence shows that the procedure was much more binding in the nineteenth century. In contemporary practice, with the various modern deviations which have been adopted, the process tends to be quite unpredictable. This is particularly true of instrumental performances, when much licence is allowed in the interest of a colourful display of virtuosity. Yet it would not be incorrect to say that still an overall move from low to high, in the arrangement of pieces within a *dastgāh*, remains the norm.

Microtone

The term microtone is generally used to denote intervals which are significantly smaller than a semi-tone. In Persian music, no such intervals are used by themselves, but I have referred to tones lowered or raised by a microtone. In such a context, a pitch may be said to be half flat or half sharp. But that may mislead us towards a notion of the quarter-tone which I would rather avoid.

Neutral 2nd

This is a very common interval in Persian music, larger than the semi-tone (minor 2nd) and smaller than the whole-tone (major 2nd), which I call the neutral 2nd. The size of this interval is unstable and may vary from about 125 cents to 170 cents, but is most commonly about 10 cents above and below the two extremes respectively (135 to 160). Often two neutral 2nds occur in succession to complete the range of a minor 3rd (295 cents). In such situations, the lower of the two tends to be the smaller (e.g. 135 + 160 = 295). The difference between the two, however, is too much subject to fluctuation to warrant separate recognition of each one, other than calling one the small neutral and the other the large neutral 2nd. A more extensive study of this interval has been given in chapter 2.

Plus 2nd

This is an interval which is larger than the major 2nd but smaller than the augmented 2nd. (The augmented 2nd is unknown in authentic Persian music.) Its size is less variable than the neutral 2nd, and is frequently in the vicinity of 270 cents (see chapter 2). In Persian modal structures, it is always preceded by a small neutral 2nd, thus the succession of the two completes the range of a major 3rd (135 + 270 = 405).

Neutral 3rd

Similar to the structure of the neutral 2nd, the neutral 3rd lies between the minor and major, varying in size from 325 to 370 cents, more often 335 to 360. It may occur as a result of the combination of a major 2nd and a neutral 2nd, or a plus 2nd and a minor 2nd. In the latter case, it will always be of the larger type close to 360 cents. In the former combination, a smaller neutral 3rd of about 335 cents will result.

Koron (p)

Koron stands for the flattening of a pitch by a microtone. This name and its symbol were devised by Ali Naqi Vaziri. Although Mr Vaziri's theories have been controversial and to a great extent refuted in recent years (chapter 2), I see no reason why this symbol and its name, which have been adopted and used widely by Persian musicians, should not be used; it is surely as good as any other, and is much more commonly understood.

Sori (⍭)

This stands for a pitch raised by a microtone, also devised by Vaziri.

4   Dastgāh-e Šur

Šur is in some respects the most important of the dastgāhs. It contains a large body of pieces, and in its domain belong at least two secondary dastgāhs, Abuatā and Dašti.[1] They will be discussed in separate chapters. A great many folk tunes, from different parts of Persia, are founded on the modal schemes of Šur or its derivative dastgāhs and gušes.

The melodic formation in Šur is conceived within the modal structure shown in example 1.

Example 1

The characteristics of this mode are:

1.   The tetrachord above the finalis is the focal point of melodic activity.
2.   The finalis is the most emphasised tone.
3.   The 4th above is the minimal high point in the mode, and has considerable prominence.
4.   The 2nd and particularly the 3rd above the finalis are also heard frequently.
5.   The 5th above is a moteqayyer. When the melodic line is descending, it is usually lowered by a microtone from a to a^p. This lowering is responsible for the creation of a sense of finalis for the 4th above, since by lowering the a^t to a^p the original tetrachord is recreated from g.
6.   The 6th above has no significant role except as a note of resolution for the 5th when used ascendingly (a^t). The 7th above can be, and frequently is, entirely omitted.
7.   The 2nd below has considerable importance both as a frequent note of āqāz and in cadences, where one of the most common cadential patterns involves a progression from the 2nd below to the finalis.
8.   The 3rd below is also used frequently in cadences. In such situations it is used ascendingly, resolving to the 2nd below and then to the finalis. Here, the 3rd below is higher than its octave (6th above) by a microtone, b^p instead of b^t.

Forud

In every dastgāh the forud assumes a very significant role as a unifying agent which binds together the various gušes in that dastgāh. In most dastgāhs, more than one forud pattern is used. In a Šur forud, the finalis may be approached a) by way of the 2nd below, b) 3rd and 2nd below, c) the 2nd above, or d) the 4th above. What precedes these approaches can be brief or extensive depending on the extent of forud improvisation. In example 2, an average length for each of the above forud types is given.

Example 2

Darāmads

The melodic movement of *Šur*, as of all *dastgāh*s and *guše*s, is overwhelmingly diatonic. No leaps larger than a perfect 4th are made. Most leaps of 4ths actually occur between the end of one phrase and the beginning of another. In other situations, an upward leap of a 4th is relatively common, from the 2nd below to the 3rd above the finalis, at the beginning of a phrase (see (a) in example 5). An upward and then downward leap of a 4th is common in the *forud* (d) as shown above. This type of ending is also used in a number of other *dastgāh*s (e.g. *Homāyun* and *Navā*). The very final portion of this *forud*, which involves the leap of a 4th down, is known as *Bāl-e Kabutar* (pigeon's wing) (see example 3)[2]. Leaps of 3rds between the

Example 3

notes of the main tetrachord are used sparingly, generally in sequential and ornamental passages (example 4).

Example 4

To illustrate the melodic character of *Šur*, as represented by the *darāmad*, two different formulae for *darāmad*s of *Šur* are transcribed in example 5. These formulae, as the basis for

Example 5

improvisation, have been arrived at after analysis of numerous improvisations in *dastgāh-e Šur*. Example 6 (p. 122) is a transcription of an extended improvisation on these formulae.

After the *darāmad* section, those *gušes* which are part of the organisation of *dastgāh-e Šur* are performed. A complete *radif*, such as that of *Musā Ma'rufi*,[3] contains much redundancy and several short and insignificant pieces. The present study has been concerned with larger and more singular pieces, most of which would be included in a normal but extended performance of *Šur*.

Not included in this chapter on *Šur*, nor in chapters on other *dastgāh*s, are short pieces which are discussed collectively under the generic title of *tekke* in chapter 16. These *tekke*s, e.g. *Kerešme, Bastenegār, Zangule, Hazin*, etc., can be freely placed in various parts of a *dastgāh*, as individual pieces, or as brief improvisations in the course of the presentation of a much larger piece (*guše*).

The main *gušes* of *dastgāh-e Šur* are the following: *Salmak, Mollā Nāzi, Golriz, Bozorg, Xārā, Qajar, Ozzāl, Šahnāz, Qarače, Hoseyni, Bayāt-e Kord* and *Gereyli*. They may be performed in that order, but the order is by no means fixed. In a given performance of *dastgāh-e Šur* some of the *gušes* may be left out altogether, and the order of those included may also vary. This observation will hold true in all of the *dastgāh*s. The order in which the *gušes* are listed and described represents, at best, the most common arrangement of the most noteworthy pieces in each *dastgāh*.

Zirkaš-e Salmak and *Salmak*

These two pieces combine to make a *guše* of *Šur* which always begins in the area of the second tetrachord and, in a gradual descending movement, conclude their melodic phrases in the first tetrachord on the finalis of *Šur*. The emphasis is on the 4th, 5th and 6th above. The 5th above fluctuates between its natural and lowered forms. As a rule, at the beginning of each phrase the natural and later the lowered version are used.

In the phrase shown in example 7, were it not for the use of a♮ at the beginning, we would

Example 7

merely have duplicated the tetrachord of *Šur* from the 4th above. However, the very presence of a♮, and its subsequent change to a♭, contributes to the particular modal quality of *Salmak*. The basic melodic formula for *Zirkaš-e Salmak* is as shown in example 8. Example 9 (p. 122) is

Example 8

an improvisation in *Zirkaš-e Salmak*. The basic melodic formula for *Salmak* is given in example 10, and an improvisation based on it is shown in example 11 (p. 123).

Example 10

Mollā Nāzi

The mode and the characteristics of *Šur* are basically maintained in *guše Mollā Nāzi*. The melodic line in *Mollā Nāzi* moves to a higher register than in a *Šur darāmad*. The 5th above the finalis, which continues to be *moteqayyer*, and the 6th above, receive much emphasis.

The basic melodic formula for *Mollā Nāzi* is given in example 12, and an improvisation on this melodic idea is given in example 13 (p. 123).

Example 12

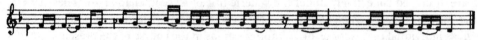

At this point a group of *guše*s are commonly played which involve a key modulation to the 4th above, but bring about no modal change. To this group belong *Golriz*, *Bozorg* and *Xārā*.

The 5th above in *Golriz* is established in its lowered form, and the 4th above functions as a new finalis, thus reproducing the *Šur* tetrachord from the 4th degree (example 14). The most

Example 14

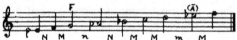

marked difference between this *guše* and *Šur* itself, aside from the change of key which is melodically of no particular significance, is that the melodic formation of *Golriz* must include the 5th above (d) which is not lowered; whereas, in *Šur* the 5th above can be left out altogether. The 6th above, also, is more prominent here, and may act as the *āqāz*. The melodic basis for *Golriz* is given in example 15, and example 16 (p. 123) is an improvisation based on it.

Example 15

Bozorg

Similar to *Golriz*, *Bozorg* employs the pentachord of *Šur* constructed on the 4th above the original finalis. As in *Golriz*, the 5th degree of this pentachord is not a *moteqayyer*. Furthermore, in *Bozorg* it becomes the note of *šāhed*. The basic melodic formula for *Bozorg* is shown in example 17. An improvisation on such a short melodic idea, however, can be lengthy, and may be developed into the kind of piece illustrated by example 18 (p. 123).

Example 17

Xārā

This *guše* is also in the new key, but, like *Šur*, it stays mostly within the range of a tetrachord. Its basic formula is as shown in example 19, and an improvisation utilising this idea is found in example 20 (p. 124).

Example 19

Qajar

The similarity between *Xārā* and *Qajar* is very striking. In fact, *Qajar* scarcely seems to be more than a variant of *Xārā*. The basic melodic formula cannot be different, as a transcribed improvisation in *Qajar*, shown in example 21 (p. 124), appears to be based on the same descending movement within the tetrachord of *Šur*.

It is important to note here that in a *dastgāh*, pieces of nearly the same structure and melodic form very frequently appear side by side with different names. In a systematic classification, one must group these pieces under the genre of one *guše*, preferably with one title, although this may be in conflict with the traditional classification.

It must also be mentioned that it is by no means unusual to find classical musicians disagreeing on the names for these pieces. For example, it would be quite in character if, in the repertoire of a certain musician, both *Xārā* and *Qajar*, as given above, were called by one of the two names, or to find that the titles have been interchanged.

Ozzāl

Ozzāl marks a return to the original key, but an octave higher. The use of the higher octave is not a matter of choice; it is the standard procedure. Traditionally, a performance of a *dastgāh* begins in a relatively low sound register and with the progress of the *dastgāh*, the register is moved upward. Thus, the *gušes* just considered move the finalis to the 4th degree above, and not the 5th below which presumably is the same note. Also, with *Ozzāl* a move is made to the key of the 8th above and not to the original key. I believe this has evolved out of the vocal tradition, where the singer always begins in the low register. As he or she warms up, the higher register (*ōj*) becomes easier to reach. Also, the greater display of virtuosity, associated by singing in the high register, is saved for the ending, which makes a greater impact on the listener.[4]

Ozzāl has a more extended melodic formula than some of the *gušes* discussed earlier. Its melodic basis is given in example 22. Example 23 (p. 32) is an improvisation on this formula.

Example 22

Ozzāl is one of the *gušes* of *Šur* which is also used in some of the other *dastgāhs*. It is often used in *dastgāh-e Homāyun*, in which case the mode of *Šur*, as well as the above melodic formula, is preserved, and therefore, a modulation from the mode of *Homāyun* to *Šur* is effected.

Šahnāz

Šahnāz is one of the most important *gušes* of *Šur*. In its mode, it does not deviate from *Šur*, but it modulates to the key of the 4th above. The melodic basis for *Šahnāz* allows for a more extensive range of sound. Improvisations in *Šahnāz* are therefore more dynamic and more intense than those in *Šur* itself, as shown in the *darāmads*. *Šahnāz* is thus regarded as an emotional *guše*, whereas a *darāmad* of *Šur* is relatively placid.

The basic melodic formula of *Šahnāz* is given in example 24, and an improvisation on this melodic pattern may be seen in example 25 (p. 125).

Example 24

Qarače

Qarače is in the same mode and tone area as *Šahnāz*, but it is melodically much more static. Its identifying characteristic lies in repeated back and forth movements between adjacent notes of the tetrachord. The basic pattern of *Qarače* can be reduced to the formula shown in example 26, and an extended improvisation on its pattern is illustrated by example 27 (p. 125).

Example 26

Hoseyni

One of the most important *gušes* of *Šur* is *Hoseyni*, which is usually performed near the end in the original key of *Šur*. In a vocal performance it would be in the original key, but at an octave above the finalis. It has a clear melodic identity that sets it apart from so many of the *gušes* which do not present any striking difference from the *darāmads* of *Šur*. *Hoseyni*'s singularity is largely due to the more ascending movement of its melodic pattern, whereas nearly all of the other *gušes* overwhelmingly support a descending melodic direction. Yet, the range of *Hoseyni* can be still confined to the first tetrachord plus the 2nd below the finalis.

The basic melodic pattern in *Hoseyni* is shown in example 28. An improvisation in *Hoseyni* is represented by the transcription shown in example 29 (p. 126).

Example 28

Hoseyni is also performed in *dastgāh-e Navā*. Its melodic character and style remain the same and it retains the mode of *Šur*.

Bayāt-e Kord

The most distinctive and independent of *gušes* performed as a part of *dastgāh-e Šur* is *Bayāt-e Kord*. Some musicians have even considered it as a separate *dastgāh* or sub-*dastgāh* inasmuch as *Dašti* and *Abustā* are given that distinction. However, since the contemporary tradition recognises only twelve *dastgāh*s, and *Bayāt-e Kord* is not one of them, and since it is usually performed as a part of *Šur* or *Dašti* (itself a sub-*dastgāh* of *Šur*), it should be considered here and not in a separate chapter.

In its mode, *Bayāt-e Kord* shows peculiarities not shared by *Šur*. The modal scheme for *Bayāt-e Kord* is given in example 30. The characteristics of this mode are:

Example 30

1. The 5th above the finalis of *Šur* is never lowered in *Bayāt-e Kord* and becomes the point of melodic concentration. As such, it is to be regarded as the *šāhed*.
2. The 4th above the finalis of *Šur* is the *āqāz*.
3. The 3rd above is the *ist*. This degree is saved for phrase endings and does not figure prominently in the course of melodic improvisation.
4. In the scale shown in example 30, a is the *šāhed*; b♭, c and g, in that order are the next most frequently heard tones.
5. The d and e♭ are occasionally used when the melodic line moves up beyond the octave. The use of e♭ instead of e^p is another peculiarity of this sound register. In the high register, there is a tendency to shrink a descending neutral 2nd to a minor 2nd, when it is a non-essential interval in the mode; this change tends to create an added element of tension. This practice is not limited to *Bayāt-e Kord*, it is also used in most of the other modes.
6. In *Bayāt-e Kord*, the finalis of *Šur* can be left out entirely. Yet, neither the *ist* nor the *šāhed* function as a satisfying finalis. Although several pieces can be improvised in the mode of *Bayāt-e Kord*, a forud in *Šur*, at the end of the last piece, seems essential for achieving a genuine feeling of conclusion. This is, perhaps, the only real justification for considering *Bayāt-e Kord* as a part of *Šur*.

The basic melodic formula for *Bayāt-e Kord* is given in example 31, and an extended improvisation is shown in example 32 (p. 126).

Example 31

A number of other pieces in the mode of *Bayāt-e Kord*, but with proper names of their own, usually follow (e.g. *Rāh-e Ruh* and *Majles Afruz*). However, the similarities between these pieces are such that their separate consideration is not warranted.

Gereyli

Probably of folk origin, *Gereyli* is a very popular *guše* usually included in the performance of *Šur*. It is in a regular duple meter and has a relatively fixed melody which is not subject to excessive variation in the course of improvisation. Its length, however, can vary according to the number of sequential additions to the fixed phrases.

The note of *āqāz* for *Gereyli* is the 3rd above the finalis of *Šur*, which is reminiscent of *Dašti* (see chapter 6). The 5th above, as in *Šur*, is *moteqayyer*, but it has much more prominence here than it does in *Šur*. This fact also recalls *Dašti* to mind. The most frequently used tone is the 4th above, but it does not dominate so consistently for it to be considered the *šāhed*. The finalis is that of *Šur*.

Because of the relative stability of *Gereyli*'s melodic form and its multiplicity of phrases, a basic skeletal formula for *Gereyli* cannot be given. Instead, a complete but brief version of *Gereyli* is offered in example 33 (p. 127).

5   *Dastgāh-e Abuatā*

Dastgāh-e Abuatā is clearly related to *Šur*. Its melodic formation is based on the modal scheme shown in example 34.

Example 34

The characteristics of *Abuatā* are the following:

1. The finalis is that of *Šur*, but it is little emphasised in the course of the melodic improvisation.
2. The 2nd above the finalis is the *ist*, and may also act as the *āqāz*.
3. The 4th above is the *šāhed*, and may also act as the *āqāz*.
4. The 5th above is not *moteqayyer* as in *Šur*, and is a non-essential tone.
5. The 2nd below the finalis is non-essential, only used in cadences when it resolves upwards to the finalis.
6. Most of the melodic activity takes place between the 2nd and the 4th above, with the 3rd above receiving frequent emphasis, but mostly as a passing tone.

Despite the above peculiarities, *Abuatā*'s dependence on *Šur* is affirmed, above all, by virtue of the fact that it does not possess separate *forud* patterns. The *forud* used in *Abuatā* is that of *Šur*, with the same finalis. Although the 2nd above takes on a prominent role, the intervals of the tetrachord above the finalis are identical with those of *Šur*. The 5th above, which is *moteqayyer* in *Šur* and not in *Abuatā*, is in either case a non-essential tone.

This is not to say, however, that *Abuatā* sounds like *Šur*. The very emphasis on the 2nd above the finalis is sufficient to change markedly the character of the mode. In addition, *Abuatā* has its own melodic patterns. The melodic movement is overwhelmingly step-wise. There are no leaps larger than thirds except between phrases.

Darāmads

The *darāmad* area of *Abuatā*, as in every other *dastgāh*, is the main body of the *dastgāh*. Several pieces under the general term of *darāmad* are performed at the outset. The basic formula around which improvisations take place is shown in example 35, and an improvisation on the *Abuatā* theme is shown in example 36 (p. 128).

Example 35

Important and commonly performed *guše*s of *Abuatā* are *Sayaxi*, *Hejāz*, *Čahār Bāq* and *Gabri*. Such *tekke*s as *Kerešme*, *Bastenegār* and *Dobeyti* are performed freely when and where the performer may wish (see chapter 16).

Sayaxi

There are no modal distinctions in *Sayaxi*; it is clearly a continuation of *Abuatā* retaining all of its characteristics. *Sayaxi*'s skeletal melodic formula, however, is somewhat different, and can be condensed into the formula shown in example 37. An improvisation on this pattern is represented by the transcription shown in example 38 (p. 128).

Example 37

Hejāz

An integral part of *Abuatā*, *Hejāz* is an extensive *guše*, no less important than *Abuatā* itself. In the *maqāmāt* system of Turko-Arabian music, *Hejāz* is an important *maqām* widely used from Turkey to Morocco. The characteristics of *Abuatā* no longer hold true in *Hejāz*, which has its own modal characteristics, as well as a very distinctive melodic pattern which cannot be confused with *Abuatā*. The melodic formation in *Hejāz* is based on the modal scheme given in example 39.

Example 39

The characteristics of *Hejāz* are the following:

1.   The finalis of *Šur* is the finalis also of *Hejāz*.
2.   The 5th above is the *šāhed* and the *ist*.
3.   Most of the melodic activity takes place between the 4th and the 8th above, although in the *forud* area, the first tetrachord is also employed.
4.   The 6th above, in the climactic portion of *Hejāz*, when leading upward, is raised by a half-step (in the scale shown in example 39 b♭ to b). This, however, is such a specific situation that the definition *moteqayyer* is not applicable to it.
5.   Leaps of a 4th (between the 4th and the 7th above) and a 5th (between the finalis and the 5th above) are occasionally encountered. The latter leap is often an aspect of the opening melodic pattern in *Hejāz*.

We see, then, that the similarity between *Hejāz* and *Abuatā* is limited to having the same finalis and using the *forud*s of *Šur*. Why is *Hejāz* a part of *Abuatā* and not vice versa? The reason, again, lies in the traditional appeal of a rise in pitch level, which makes it desirable for *Hejāz* to follow *Abuatā* and not precede it; and accordingly, the title of the opening piece is applied to the *dastgāh*. *Hejāz* shifts the centre of melodic activity to a higher register than

Abuatā. Furthermore, it is more expansive in its phrases; improvisations in *Hejāz* can cover the range of a minor 10th, which is quite unusual, in a single piece, in Persian music.[1] The use of a higher register of sound, the use of a wide range, and relatively large leaps, all combine to make *Hejāz* into one of the most striking and exciting of *gušes* in the *radif* of Persian music.

The basic melodic pattern in *Hejāz* is shown in example 40. An extended improvisation in

Example 40

Hejāz, showing the overall range of a minor 10th mentioned above, is given in example 41 (p. 128).

With the introduction of *Hejāz*, as if it were a separate *dastgāh*, a group of pieces in the form of *darāmad* are performed, all of which employ the melodic ideas in example 40. This quasi-*darāmad* section is followed by a number of *gušes* which are modally related to *Hejāz* and not to *Abuatā*. Of these, *Čahār Bāq* and *Gabri* are the most important.

Čahār Bāq

This *guše* establishes a slow and loose, but more or less stable, triple metre. The performance of this *guše* is much more characteristic of vocal than instrumental music. It is sung to a specific poem which is much loved by Persians. Having a fairly stable rhythmic organisation as well as a fixed poetic base, *Čahār Bāq* does not become subject to any significant melodic variation from one performance to another.

The melodic base of *Čahār Bāq* is the same as that of *Hejāz*. In fact, it appears to be a mere variation, in a set metre, on the theme of *Hejāz*, with the same characteristics.

For a transcription of *Čahār Bāq*, see example 42 (p. 129).

Gabri

Gabri is also in the mode of *Hejāz*. The same overall descending pattern from the area of *šahed* (5th above) to the finalis persists. A singular characteristic of *Gabri* is a brief ascending pattern from the 4th above to the 7th above the finalis as shown in examples 43 and 44 (for the

Example 43

latter, see p. 130). The skeletal formula for *Gabri* is as shown in example 43, and an improvisation is transcribed in example 44 (p. 130).

The conclusion of the *dastgāh-e Abuatā* is marked by an extended *forud* in *Šur*. The mode of *Abuatā* as presented at the beginning of the *dastgāh* does not necessarily return. As the last pieces are all in the mode of *Hejāz* with the *forud* in *Šur*, a re-establishment of *Abuatā* is not effected. We see that in the manner of its conclusions also, *dastgāh-e Abuatā* seems to show its dependence on *dastgāh-e Šur*.

6   Dastgāh-e Dašti

Another *dastgāh* related to *dastgāh-e Šur* is *Dašti*, which, like *Abuatā* and *Hejāz*, makes use of the *forud*s of *Šur*. As such, single pieces in *Dašti*, as well as the *dastgāh* itself, conclude in the mode of *Šur*. Apart from the *forud* area, however, *Dašti* relies on melodic ideas distinct from *Šur*. *Dašti* melodies are conceived within the modal scheme shown in example 45.

Example 45

The characteristics of *Dašti* are the following:

1. The finalis of *Šur* and *Dašti* is the same note. It assumes prominence only in the *forud*.
2. The 2nd above the finalis is non-essential.
3. The 3rd above is most commonly the *āqāz*.
4. The 4th above has very frequent usage, and may occasionally act as the *āqāz*.
5. The 5th above is the *šahed*, as well as the *moteqayyer*. It is lowered often by a microtone (a to a^P, in the above scale) when descending to the 4th.
6. The 6th and 7th above are used less frequently than the 5th and the 4th, but are essential tones in the formation of *Dašti* melodies.
7. The 8th above constitutes the normal high point and is used at climactic portions of the melody.
8. Most of the melodic activity takes place between the 3rd and the 7th above.
9. The melodic movement is primarily step-wise. Leaps of thirds are common, and the leap of a fourth is occasionally used between the 4th and the 7th above.

Darāmads

Dastgāh-e Dašti proper as represented by its *darāmad*s, is based on a very distinctive melodic pattern which becomes subject to innumerable variations. This theme, exhibiting the above characteristics, in its basic unembellished form, is as given in example 46. As the *darāmad*

Example 46

section of *Dašti* may be lengthy and very flexible, two examples of *darāmad* improvisations on the two ideas shown in example 46 are given in examples 47 and 48 (see pp. 130 and 131).

Dastgāh-e Dašti does not contain many *gušes*, and the few that there are do not show much difference of character from the *darāmads*. In fact, some of the *gušes* seem to be no more than further variations on the main theme (see example 46). Thus, the initial charm of *Dašti* gradually gives way to uniformity and monotony.

The *gušes* of *Dašti* are *Bidagāni*, *Čupāni*, *Daštestāni*, *Qamangiz*, *Gilaki*, *Kučebāqi*, and *Oššāq*. The skeletal melodic ideas for all but *Oššāq* are very little different from that of *Dašti* itself (*darāmad*s), and retain the same characteristics. In the following, the basic melodic formula for each of these *gušes* is given, followed by an improvisation on each.

Bidagāni

Basic melodic formula:

Example 49

An extended improvisation on the above is shown in example 50 (see p. 131).

Čupāni

Basic melodic formula:

Example 51

Improvisation is shown in example 52 (see p. 132).

Daštestāni

Basic melodic formula:

Example 53

Improvisation is shown in example 54 (see p. 132).

Qamangiz

Basic melodic formula:

Example 55

Improvisation is shown in example 56 (see p. 132).

Gilaki

Basic melodic formula:

Example 57

Improvisation is shown in example 58 (see p. 133).

Kučebāqi

Basic melodic formula:

Example 59

Improvisation is shown in example 60 (see p. 133).

Oššāq

With *guše-ye Oššāq*, the mode of *Dašti* is relinquished in favour of *Šur*. As we have seen, every one of the above *gušes* has ended in *Šur* by means of a *forud* of *Šur*. *Oššāq*, which is usually but not always included in the performance of *Dašti*, is in *Šur* proper. Thus, *dastgāh-e Dašti* not only concludes all of its pieces in the mode of *Šur*, but like *Abuatā*, provides us with a piece strictly in the mode of *Šur* for the conclusion of the *dastgāh*.

As indicated in the case of *Hejāz*, *Oššāq* is also an important *maqām* in the Turko-Arabian musical tradition, and has wide usage throughout the Middle East and North Africa.

In *Oššāq*, the 4th above the finalis of *Šur* becomes the *šāhed* which recalls *Abuatā* to mind. The *āqāz* is not stable, and there is no *ist*. As in the case of *Šur* itself, *Oššāq* does not employ a wide range of sound. The main melodic formula is contained within the range of a pentachord, from the 2nd below the 4th above the finalis. But, in the course of an improvisation, this range may be extended.

The basic melodic formula for *Oššāq* is given in example 61, and the transcription of an improvisation in example 62 (see p. 134).

Example 61

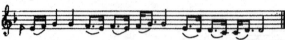

Oššāq is one of a few *gušes* which appear in more than one *dastgāh* without any significant change in their modal and melodic structure. In the case of *tekke*s, discussed in chapter 16, I shall show that all such short pieces which appear in different *dastgāh*s, while preserving their melodic identity, yield to the mode of the *dastgāh* in which they are placed. *Oššāq* and a few other *gušes*, which will be discussed in other chapters, maintain their own modes regardless of where they are placed.

It is curious that *Oššāq*, which is in the mode of *Šur*, is not as a rule performed in *dastgāh-e Šur*. It may be played in *Homāyun*, *Bayāt-e Esfahān*, *Rāst*, or *Navā*, at least the first three of which are very distinct and distant from *Šur*. In such cases, of course, *Oššāq* must be introduced by means of a modulation to the mode of *Šur*.

In concluding this chapter on *dastgāh-e Dašti*, it is important to mention that *Dašti* has strong links with the rural music of Persia. An overwhelming number of folk songs, especially those from the Caspian Sea littoral, and many from the *Fārs* region, are in the mode of *Dašti*. It is the most natural thing for a Persian shepherd to play on his pipe in the mode of *Dašti*, or for farmers, returning to the village from the fields, to sing impromptu melodies in *Dašti*. Although the folk music of Persia does not lie within the scope of this book, it is appropriate at this point to give an example of one folk song which is clearly in the mode and within the melodic framework of *Dašti*. This folk song is from the northern province of Gilān (see example 63).

Example 63

7   Dastgāh-e Bayāt-e Tork

The meaning of the word *Bayāt* is uncertain. It may be an abbreviated form of *Abyāt*, meaning stanzas. The word *Tork* (Turk), on the other hand, is clear enough. Yet, in connection with this *dastgāh*, it does not refer to the Turks of Turkestan, Azerbaijan (i.e. both Soviet and Iranian Azerbaijan) or Turkey. It is believed that many of the songs of the Turkic tribes of Southern Persia, notably the *Qašqāi*, are in this mode, and that the reference is to them. In fact, this *dastgāh* is also known by the name of *Bayāt-e Zand*, which stands for the Zand tribe (also of Turkic stock) of the Fārs region. This title, however, is not commonly used today for the *dastgāh*.

As shown in the previous two chapters, there are some bases for considering *Abuatā* and *Dašti* as satellites of *Šur*. The connection between *Bayāt-e Tork* and *Afšāri* with *Šur* seems much more tenuous, even though the tradition identifies them as derivatives of *Šur*. It is true, however, that some pieces in the collection of these two *dastgāhs* are modally close to the mode of *Šur*.

In identifying both *Bayāt-e Tork* and *Afšāri* as independent *dastgāhs*, it is of far greater importance that both have modal schemes distinct from *Šur*. Furthermore, they have *forud* patterns of their own with notes of *ist* and finalis different from those of *Šur*. In this connection, therefore, it is difficult to reconcile tradition with analytical observation.

Bayāt-e Tork has the modal scheme shown in example 64a. Its characteristics are:

Example 64a

1. The finalis and the *šāhed* are the same tone.
2. The 4th below the finalis is the *āqāz* and the *ist*.
3. Other tones in the mode in order of their importance and frequency of usage are the 2nd above, the 2nd below, the third below, the 3rd above and the 4th above the finalis.
4. Melodic formation takes place in the tetrachord from the 4th below to the finalis in an ascending order, and in the tetrachord above the finalis in a descending order. Thus, the finalis becomes a centre of melodic formation from both directions.
5. In an ornamental trill (see example 64b) on the finalis, the 2nd above is occasionally lowered

Example 64b

by a half step (g to g♭, in the scale shown in example 64a). This is peculiar to a *forud* which ends on the *ist*.

6.   In a *forud* which ends on the *ist* and not on the finalis, a leap of a neutral 3rd down, from the 2nd below to the 4th below is the norm.

Darāmads

In its *darāmad*s, *Bayāt-e Tork* displays all of the above characteristics. The basic melodic formula for a *darāmad* of *Bayāt-e Tork* is given in example 65, and an improvisation on this melodic idea is shown in example 66 (see p. 134).

Example 65

As with *Dašti*, *Bayāt-e Tork* suffers from relative uniformity. The prevalence of the *šāhed* throughout is largely responsible for a marked monotony. The main *guše*s in *Bayāt-e Tork* are *Dogāh*, *Ruholarvāh*, *Mehdizarrābi*, *Qatār* and *Qarāi*.

Dogāh

The use of the word *gāh*, which means place, in connection with this *guše*, as well as in *dastgāh*, *Segāh*, *Čahārgāh* and *Panjgāh*, cannot be satisfactorily explained. *Dastgāh* has come to mean system or organisation, and its usage is not exclusively musical. *Dogāh*, *Segāh*, *Čahārgāh* and *Panjgāh*, on the other hand, are purely musical terms which, when literally translated, indicate, respectively second place, third place, fourth place and fifth place. It is believed that this 'place', in the context of medieval music, referred to the position of the respective finals of these modes, in relation to a fundamental pitch, on the finger board of lute-type instruments. In contemporary usage, however, no such relationships can be satisfactorily established. There is no fundamental pitch; and the modes represented by these 'places' do not have a two-three-four-five relationship to one another, however we may consider them.

Interestingly enough, *Segāh* and *Čahārgāh* are the names of two *dastgāh*s. *Panjgāh* is a partial name of one *dastgāh* which shall be discussed later (see chapter 15). But *Dogāh* is only a *guše* in *Bayāt-e Tork*, and does not present any significant difference from the *darāmad*s of *Bayāt-e Tork*.

The basic melodic formula of *Dogāh* is formed within the lower tetrachord, from the 4th below to the finalis, as shown in example 67. The range may, however, be slightly extended to

Example 67

the 2nd above, as seen in the transcription of an improvisation in *Dogāh* shown in example 68 (p. 135).

Ruholarvāh

With *Ruholarvāh*, a small but significant change in the mode of *Bayāt-e Tork* takes place. The 4th below the finalis loses its prominence as the *āqāz* and the *ist*. Instead the 3rd below becomes prominent, particularly as the *ist*. Consequently something of the atmosphere of the mode of *Šur* is created. The *šāhed*, however, remains the same as in the *darāmad*s, and helps maintain the feeling of *Bayāt-e Tork*. *Ruholarvāh* and *Mehdizarrābi* both seem to be hybrid *guše*s combining *Bayāt-e Tork* and *Šur*. They have, no doubt, contributed to the traditional acceptance of *Bayāt-e Tork* as a satellite of *Šur*.

In *Ruholarvāh* and *Mehdizarrābi* the modal scheme is as given in example 69. The basic

Example 69

melodic formula for *Ruholarvāh* is shown in example 70, and an extended improvisation on it is found in example 71 (p. 136).

Example 70

Mehdizarrābi

This *guše* is similar to *Ruholarvāh* and makes use of the same pentachord (see example 69). But the 2nd below the finalis of *Bayāt-e Tork* (e^p in the above scale) takes on a prominent role. *Mehdizarrābi*'s basic melodic pattern is given in example 72, and an improvisation on it in example 73 (p. 136).

Example 72

Qatār

Of all the *guše*s of *Bayāt-e Tork*, *Qatār* is the most important; it is always included in a performance of *Bayāt-e Tork*. Its melodic patterns are formed within the tetrachord below the finalis (c to f, in our scale). As with *Mehdizarrābi*, in *Qatār* the 2nd below the finalis, next to the finalis, is the most prominent note. The 4th below is the *āqāz*, as well as the *ist*. The basic melodic formula for *Qatār* is given in example 74, and an improvisation on it in example 75 (p. 137).

Example 74

Qarāi

Qarāi represents the '*ōj*' or high point in *Bayāt-e Tork*. It is performed usually near the end of the *dastgāh*. It displays modal peculiarities of its own, as shown in example 76.

Example 76

The melodic movement in *Qarāi* has a decidedly descending pattern, first in the higher tetrachord of the above scale (from c to g), and later in the lower pentachord (from g to c). Improvisations in *Qarāi*, therefore, are in two long phrases, one in each of these two areas. The range covered, including ornamental tones beyond the above octave, can be as wide as an 11th.

The *šāhed*-finalis of *Bayāt-e Tork* (f in the above scale), no longer functions in either role. In the first phrase of *Qarāi* the 8th above the finalis (c) is the *šāhed*; in the second phrase there is no discernible *šāhed*, although e^p is prominent. The finalis for *Qarāi* is the *ist* of *Bayāt-e Tork*.

The basic formulae for each of the two sections of *Qarāi* are shown in example 77. An improvisation in *Qarāi* is shown in example 78 (see p. 138).

Example 77

Similar to *Dašti*, *Bayāt-e Tork* has wide application in the folk music of Persia. Particularly among the Kurds of the west, and the Turkic tribes of the north-west and the south, folk songs in the mode of *Bayāt-e Tork* are common.

8   Dastgāh-e Afšāri

As with *Bayāt-e Tork*, *Afšāri* possesses modal characteristics distinct from *Šur*. However, the final *gušes* in *Afšāri* often modulate to the mode of *Šur*, and the *dastgāh* may in fact conclude in *Šur*. This, no doubt, has been responsible for the traditional belief that *Afšāri* is a satellite of *dastgāh-e Šur*.

Certainly, in the *darāmad*s of the *dastgāh*, there can be no confusion with *Šur*, as *Afšāri* establishes its own modal and melodic character, as well as its own *forud* patterns.

The modal scheme in *Afšāri* is shown in example 79. The characteristics of this mode are as follows:

Example 79

1.   The finalis is used very sparingly. In the course of melodic improvisation it can be avoided altogether, being saved only for the very last note.
2.   The 2nd above the finalis is a non-essential tone and can be omitted.
3.   The 3rd above is the *ist*. Nearly all the melodic phrases, and even some of the pieces, end on the *ist*.
4.   The 4th above is a passing tone between the *ist* and the *šāhed* (5th above) and is much used, but does not take on a specific role.
5.   The 5th above is the *šāhed*, as well as the usual *āqāz*.
6.   The 6th above is *moteqayyer*, but its basic form is the lowered one (a^p in the above scale). It is occasionally raised by a microtone (a^k).
7.   The 7th and the 8th above are non-essential in the *darāmad*s, but are emphasised in some of the ensuing *gušes*, to be discussed later.

At a glance, these modal characteristics may seem somewhat close to *Šur*, and it would appear that the traditional classification is not far from correct. In particular, the similarity to the mode of *Abuatā*, itself a satellite of *Šur*, is striking. However, the fact that the *moteqayyer* in *Afšāri* is mostly in its lowered form whereas in *Šur* it is mostly in its raised form, the fact that the finalis of *Šur* in the *darāmad*s of *Afšāri* is non-essential, and the fact that *Afšāri* presents its own *forud* patterns, all combine to give this *dastgāh* qualities not shared by *Šur*.

Ali Naqi Vaziri[1] and his disciple, Ruhollāh Xāleqi,[2] are also of the opinion that *Afšāri* is independent of *Šur*. They are more inclined to accept it as a derivative of *Segāh*, the *dastgāh* that is the subject of chapter 9.

The most representative *forud* pattern in *Afšāri* can be illustrated by example 80. Three significant observations on this pattern may be made:

Example 80

1.   The 4th above the finalis (f) is used in an ornamental fashion, often with a trill, not to g, but g♭. A similar trill, from f to g♭, was noted in the *forud* to the *ist* in *Bayāt-e Tork* (example 64b).

2.   The 2nd above is omitted, and a skip of a neutral third from the 3rd above to the finalis is made.

3.   It is noteworthy that the finalis is heard only at the end; throughout the emphasis is on the *ist* (3rd above). In some performances even this brief reference to the finalis is omitted, thereby giving the *ist* every reason to be taken as the finalis. This, however, is more in the character of 'modern' developments. In the traditional style and in older recordings of *Afšāri*, the finalis (c in the European scale) is nearly always given for decisive conclusions.

Darāmadhā

The *darāmad* area of *Afšāri* is very extensive and embodies two types of improvisation. The initial pieces are contained within a neutral third, from the 5th to the 3rd above the finalis, mostly in a descending movement. The 6th above is also used, and occasionally, when the phrase exceeds that degree and goes to the 7th, the 6th is raised by a microtone (a^p to a). When descending, it is again lowered, and is resolved on the *šāhed* (5th above).

The basic formula for this type of *darāmad* of *Afšāri* is shown in example 81. A transcription of an improvisation on this formula is shown in example 82 (p. 138).

Example 81

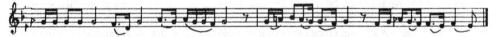

A number of improvisations in this area of the mode are usually followed by an extension of the range to cover the 7th, 8th and 9th above the finalis, with considerable emphasis on the higher register. In most *dastgāh*s, such a change would represent a new *guše*, but in *Afšāri*, this shift of emphasis to the higher register of the mode is simply an extension of the *darāmad*s. The concluding portion of this type of *darāmad*, however, marks a return to the area of *šāhed* and *ist*, that is the lower register.

The basic formula for this type of *darāmad* is shown in example 83. In this register, because

Example 83

of the frequent use of the 7th and 8th above, and the generally upward movement of each phrase, the use of the raised 6th shown here is much more characteristic than in the first type of *darāmad*. An improvisation on this formula is shown in example 84 (see p. 139).

Whereas the *darāmad* area of *Afšāri* is quite distinctive and extensive, the *guše*s that follow are few and are mostly from the repertoire of other *dastgāh*s. These *guše*s are *Bayāt-e Rāje'*, *Rohāb*, *Masihi*, *Nahib* and *Masnavi Pič*.

Bayāt-e Rāje'

Guše-ye Bayāt-e Rāje' is also performed in *dastgāh-e Bayāt-e Esfahān* and in *dastgāh-e Navā*. Its modal characteristics make it more natural to those two *dastgāh*s than to *Afšari*. Its discussion shall be deferred, therefore, to the chapter on *Bayāt-e Esfahān* (chapter 12). Here, may it suffice to say that in *Bayāt-e Rāje'*, the 6th above the finalis of *Afšari* is raised (a¹), and as such it remains fixed. Furthermore, that degree becomes the *šahed*, while the 5th above becomes the *ist*.

Rohāb

Rohāb is in the mode of *Šur*, and it is also performed in *dastgāh-e Šur* and in *Bayāt-e Esfahān*. However, it is performed in *Afšari* more often than in the other two *dastgāh*s. Here, the finalis of *Šur* (d, the 2nd above in the scale of *Afšari*), assumes a prominent role as the finalis. All the other characteristics of *Šur* are also present.

The basic melodic formula for *Rohāb* is given in example 85, and an improvisation on it is shown in example 86 (see p. 139).

Example 85

Masihi

Masihi is also in the mode of *Šur*. The word *Masihi*, meaning Christian (followers of the Messiah), is certainly baffling. It may also be performed in *dastgāh-e Navā*. The inclusion of *Rohāb* and *Masihi*, which are in the mode of *Šur*, in *dastgāh-e Afšari*, has no doubt helped the notion that *Afšari* is a derivative of *Šur*.

The basic melodic formula for *Masihi* is shown in example 87. For an improvisation in *Masihi*, see example 88 (p. 140).

Example 87

Nahib

Nahib and two other related *guše*s (*Arāq, Āšur*) present a distinct mode of their own. In *Afšari*, only *Nahib* is performed. But in *Māhur, Rāst* and *Navā*, usually all three are played. Particularly in *Māhur*, considerable emphasis is placed on these *guše*s, and they are above all identified with the structure of that *dastgāh*. All three will be covered in the discussion of *Dastgāh-e Māhur* in chapter 14.

It should be mentioned here that the finalis of *Afšari* (c) is also the finalis for *Nahib*. The 8th above is the *šahed* and the 5th above is the *ist*.

Masnavi Pič

This *guše* will be discussed in chapter 16. It is an essential part of *Afšāri*. Certainly a vocal rendition of this *dastgāh* would not be complete without *Masnavi Pič*. For a transcription of it, see example 329 (p. 188).

9 Dastgāh-e Segāh

Similarities between the modes of *Segāh* and *Afšāri* are so striking that it would seem reasonable to consider the two as manifestations of a single modal structure. Yet, for the reasons already discussed (chapter 8), *Afšāri* is traditionally considered to be related to *Šur*. While theoretically the similarities between *Segāh* and *Afšāri* are of interest, in practice the two are not associated or confused with one another.

The modal scheme in *Segāh*, which at first glance may seem identical with *Afšāri*, can be seen in example 89. The characteristics of this mode are as follows:

Example 89

1. The finalis, the *šahed* and the most frequent *āqāz* are the same note. This points to the overriding significance of this note in the mode.
2. The 2nd above the finalis is frequently used, but mostly as a passing tone between the finalis and the 3rd.
3. The 3rd above, after the finalis, is the most prominent note.
4. The 4th above defines the minimal upper register of the mode, which, in relationship to the finalis, establishes the *Segāh* tetrachord.
5. The 3rd below is important in the *forud* area, when a leap of a neutral 3rd from that note to the finalis is very typical.
6. The 5th and the 6th above are non-essential, and the 2nd below can be omitted altogether.
7. The mode of *Segāh* is entirely made of neutral and whole-tone intervals; there are no semi-tones.

Forud

The *forud* patterns of *Segāh* are very distinct from those of *Afšāri*. The ending neutral 3rd leap is ascending in *Segāh* but descending in *Afšāri*; the finalis is also different. The 4th above in *Segāh* (a^p), corresponding to the 6th above in *Afšāri*, is not *moteqayyer*. And, the 5th above in *Afšāri* (g), corresponding to the 3rd above in *Segāh*, has a more prominent role. That note in *Afšāri* is the *šahed*, as well as the most common *āqāz*.

The most representative *forud* pattern in *Segāh* is shown in example 90.

Example 90

Darāmads

In the *darāmad* area, the *Segāh* proper is presented within the range of the tetrachord from the finalis to the 4th above. The 3rd below the finalis also figures prominently at the beginning of each piece, and particularly in the *forud*.

The basic melodic formula for a *darāmad* of *Segāh* can be seen in example 91, and an improvisation on the formula is shown in example 92 (see p. 140).

Example 91

After the *darāmad* area, which includes several improvisations on the above melodic idea, we come to the *gušes* of *dastgāh-e Segāh*. A curious fact about these *gušes* is that every one of them is, or can be, also performed in *dastgāh-e Čahārgāh* and in the mode of *Čahārgāh*. Interestingly enough, the modes and the aesthetics of *Segāh* and *Čahārgāh* are not at all similar. Here, we shall discuss these *gušes* as they appear in *Segāh*, and in the following chapter it shall be shown how these pieces are adapted to the structure of *Čahārgāh*.

The main *gušes* of *dastgāh-e Segāh* are *Zang-e Šotor*, *Zābol*, *Muye*, *Hesār*, *Moxālef* and *Maqlub*.

Zang-e Šotor

This *guše* has a very unusual melodic shape, as it is conceived around a few long sustained notes separated by a 'pedal point', with a regular pattern of embellishment on the long notes. The pedal point is the 3rd below and the melodic pattern begins with the finalis in a slow step-wise progression up to the 4th above and back to the finalis. In essence, *Zang-e Šotor* simply outlines the mode of *Segāh* in its most basic form.

The basic melodic formula for *Zang-e Šotor* is shown in example 93. *Zang-e Šotor* with improvised ornaments is shown in example 94 (p. 141).

Example 93

Zābol

The change of modal character from *Segāh*, as shown in the *darāmads*, to *guše-ye Zābol* is slight. The 3rd above in the *darāmads* is after the finalis, the most important tone; in *Zābol*, this tone becomes the *šāhed*, and is very much the centre of melodic activity. The finalis is less prominent and is heard mostly at the beginning and at the end of phrases. The melodic formation is still limited, in essence, to the tetrachord of the finalis to the 4th above. Therefore, the change introduced by *Zābol* is merely a shift of emphasis from the finalis to the 3rd above.

The basic melodic formula for *Zābol* can be seen in example 95, and the transcription of an improvisation in it is shown in example 96 (p. 141).

Example 95

Muye

In *guše-ye Muye*, the centre of melodic activity is raised higher to the area of the 3rd to the 5th above the finalis. This creates a more notable change from the mode of *Segāh* than the change provided by *Zābol*. The 5th above, which so far has been only a peripheral tone, is now very important. The finalis and the 2nd above lose their prominence, and are heard only in the *forud*. The mode of *Muye*, therefore, takes on the scheme given in example 97a.

Example 97a

In *Muye*, within the range of a minor third, from g to b♭ in the above scale, all three tones receive almost equal emphasis.

The basic formula for *Muye* is given in example 97b. An improvisation on this skeletal idea can be seen in example 98 (p. 142).

Example 97b

Hesār

Both in *Segāh* and *Čahārgāh* (as shall be seen in the next chapter), *Hesār* involves a modulation to the 'key' a perfect 5th above the finalis of the original model of the *dastgāh*. In *Segāh*, the 5th above in relation to the finalis is not perfect, but is half-diminished (e^p to b♭ in our scale of *Segāh*). The 5th above is therefore raised to b^p, and as such it becomes the finalis of a new *Segāh* mode (see example 99).

Example 99

While the scale of *Hesār*, as shown in example 99, is identical in structure with that of *Segāh* itself, its modal characteristics are somewhat different:

1. The 3rd below is often the *āqāz*.
2. The 2nd below is much more frequently heard than the 2nd below in the mode of *Segāh*.

3.   The 2nd above, after the finalis, is the most prominent tone.
4.   The 3rd and the 4th above have less prominence than in the mode of *Segāh*.

The basic formula for *Hesār* can be seen in example 100, and an improvisation in example 101 (p. 142).

Example 100

Moxālef

Both *Moxālef* and *Maqlub* are in a new mode which is surprisingly remote from the original mode of *Segāh*. This new mode is very close to the mode of *Bayāt-e Esfahān*, which will be discussed in chapter 12. In relation to the mode of *Hesār*, however, which establishes the mode of *Segāh* from a perfect 5th above the original finalis, the change to *Moxālef* is slight. The 2nd above of *Hesār* becomes the finalis of *Moxālef* and the 4th above is lowered by a microtone. The transition from *Hesār* to *Moxālef* is thus a smooth one, particularly since the 2nd above has been a prominent tone in *Hesār*, and the 4th above, which is now lowered, is a non-essential tone both in *Hesār* and in *Moxālef*.

The modal scheme for *Moxālef* can be seen in example 102[1]. The characteristics of this mode are:

Example 102

1.   The finalis and the *šāhed* are the same tone.
2.   Melodic activity centres in the area of the 4th below to the 2nd above the finalis.
3.   The 3rd below occasionally acts as the *ist*.
4.   The 4th below is the usual *āqāz*.
5.   With the use of the upper e♭, a semi-tone has finally been brought into use.

The basic melodic formula for *Moxālef* is shown in example 103, and an improvisation in example 104 (p. 142).

Example 103

Maqlub

Maqlub always follows *Moxālef*. They are similar in modal character and in melodic style. *Maqlub* represents the 'ōj' in *dastgāh-e Segāh*, and as such, presses on to a higher register not used in *Moxālef*. One might say it represents an extension of the mode of *Moxālef* with the emphasis on the tetrachord above the finalis instead of the one below it. The mode of *Maqlub* will take on the form shown in example 105.

Example 105

The characteristics of this mode are somewhat different from that of Moxālef:

1. The finalis is the *šāhed* and also the *āqāz*.
2. The 4th and the 3rd below have lost their prominence.
3. The 2nd below is important as a 'leading tone' to the finalis; it may also function as the *āqāz*.
4. The 3rd above is very prominent.
5. The 4th above, absent in the mode of *Moxālef*, is heard frequently.
6. The minor tetrachord (c–f) is the focal point (another point of strong similarity to the mode of *Bayāt-e Esfahān*).

The basic melodic formula for *Maqlub* is shown in example 106, and an improvisation on this theme is represented in example 107 (p. 143).

Example 106

Although *Maqlub* is normally the last *guše* performed in *Segāh*, it is always followed by a modulation back to the original mode and the original key. This is done by a descending pattern from the finalis of *Maqlub* to the 4th below it (g). That tone in turn becomes the *šāhed* for another improvisation in *Muye* (see *Muye*, example 98). In *Muye* the 2nd below the finalis of *Maqlub* is lowered by a microtone (b^p to b$^{\flat}$), and from there, the return to the original mode of *Segāh* for the ending is smoothly achieved. It involves no tone alterations, but a simple shift of emphasis from the *šāhed* of *Muye* (g) to the *šāhed*-finalis of *Segāh* (e^p).

This lengthy process of modulation and descent, from the high register and the distinctly separate mode of *Moxālef* to the original mode of *Segāh*, brings into sharp focus the very meaning of *forud*. In most cases a *forud* is little more than a mere melodic cadence which refers back to the modal material of the *darāmad*. Here, the *forud* is not only acting as the cadence but is also demonstrating its true meaning of 'descent', to the low register of the beginning of the *dastgāh*, requiring very discernible changes in modes.

10 *Dastgāh-e Čahārgāh*

Segāh and *Čahārgāh* are allied to a degree unparalleled in any other two *dastgāh*s. Virtually every piece performed in *Segāh* can be performed in *Čahārgāh*, although *Čahārgāh* includes a few *gušes* peculiar to that *dastgāh* and not performed in *Segāh*.

The basic modes of these two *dastgāh*s, on the other hand, appear to be as remote from one another as any two modes in Persian music can be. The mode of *Segāh* contains no minor seconds and no plus seconds. Its main tetrachord is composed of the intervals of large neutral, major second and small neutral (N-M-n), in that order. The mode of *Čahārgāh* contains two minor seconds and two plus seconds, and its main tetrachord is composed of a small neutral, a plus second and a minor second (n-P-m).

Čahārgāh's modal scheme is given in example 108. The characteristics of this mode are the following:

Example 108

1. The finalis has a central position in the mode. It is the tone which connects two conjunct tetrachords of identical structure.
2. The 3rd below the finalis is the usual *āqāz*. It is also very important in the *forud* where an upward leap of a neutral 3rd, from that tone to the finalis, is almost mandatory.
3. The 4th below is the normal bottom of the register. It is approached and left diatonically from the 3rd below.
4. The 2nd and 3rd above, and the tetrachord above the finalis in general, have a less prominent role than the tetrachord below.
5. The 4th above is the least frequently heard tone in the mode.
6. There is no *moteqayyer*.

Forud

While a marked dissimilarity of modal structure between this mode and that of *Segāh* is clearly visible, one common characteristic of the two should be emphasised. In the *forud*, which is the single most individual stamp of any *dastgāh*'s identity, both *Segāh* and *Čahārgāh* employ the concluding motif of an upward leap of a neutral 3rd, in both cases from the 3rd below to the finalis. This creates at once a common atmosphere, albeit momentary, which goes some way towards accommodating the use of the same *gušes* in both *dastgāh*s.

The example of a *Čahārgāh forud* given in example 109 shows that both the concluding motif and the whole of the phrase have a strong similarity to a *Segāh forud*. We see that the

Example 109

portion of this phrase under the bracket, in terms of interval structure, is identical with a *Segāh forud* (see example 90). The 2nd below, which is different and makes for a different interval to the finalis in each of the two modes, has been avoided. All the other intervals are the same as in *Segāh*: from the 4th below to the 3rd below is a neutral 2nd; from the 3rd below to the finalis is a neutral 3rd; and from the finalis to the 2nd above is a neutral 2nd.

It would seem, therefore, that the modes of *Segāh* and *Cahārgāh* are more reconcilable than the mere study of the two scales may suggest. And the practice of employing the same pieces in both *dastgāh*s, adapting to the modal requirements of one or the other, is not as strange as it may seem at first.

Darāmads

Although in the *darāmad* area the tetrachord below the finalis is more emphasised, the tetrachord above is also used. Thus *Cahārgāh* makes use of a wider tonal range at the outset than most other modes discussed so far. The movement is overwhelmingly diatonic, with the conspicuous exception of the leap from the 3rd below to the finalis. *Darāmad*s, being the most representative part of the *dastgāh*, fully exhibit the modal characteristics given above. The basic formula for a *darāmad* of *Cahārgāh* can be seen in example 110. An improvisation on this formula is shown in example 111 (p. 143).

Example 110

With the conclusion of the *darāmad*s, the *gušes* of *Cahārgāh* are introduced. They are *Zang-e Šotor*, *Zābol*, *Muye*, *Hesār*, *Moxālef*, *Maqlub*, *Hodi*, *Pahlavi*, *Rajaz* and *Mansuri*. All of these *gušes*, except the last four, have been seen in *dastgāh-e Segāh*. Although their melodic forms remain essentially the same, their modes are different. They will be discussed here as they appear in the *dastgāh-e Cahārgāh*.

Zang-e Šotor

The use of this *guše* in *Cahārgāh* is not as common as it is in *Segāh*. When used, it is almost identical in composition to the *Zang-e Šotor* given in *Segāh*. The 'pedal point' is the 3rd below, and the melody merely consists of the tones of the tetrachord above the finalis. The embellishments on these tones can be different, inasmuch as a free improvisation is likely to make that possible. The basic difference between a *Zang-e Šotor* in *Segāh* and one in *Cahārgāh* is, therefore, in the very structure of the two tetrachords. The basic melodic formula is shown in example 112. An improvisation in *Zang-e Šotor* of *Cahārgāh* is represented by example 113 (p. 144).

Example 112

Zābol

Just as in *dastgāh-e Segāh*, *Zābol* brings about a subtle change of character in the mode of *Čahārgāh*. Not only does the 3rd above become the *šāhed*, but the tetrachord below the finalis, which was very much a focal point in the *darāmad*s, is no longer heard. The latter development accounts for a more striking change in *Čahārgāh* than it does in *Segāh*, where the tetrachord below the finalis does not assume any significance in the *darāmad* area. The finalis loses its prominence and is heard only at the beginning and at the conclusion of the piece.

The modal scheme of *Zābol* in *Čahārgāh* is therefore as given in example 114a, and its

Example 114a

melodic formula can be seen in example 114b. Example 115 (p. 145) gives an improvisation on this thematic idea, and also shows the finalis at the beginning and the end.

Example 114b

Muye

It has been noted that in *Segāh*, *Muye* concentrates in the area of the 3rd to the 5th above. In *Čahārgāh*, the same transition takes place. At the same time, the 5th above is lowered by a microtone, so that the interval between the 4th and the 5th is changed from a major 2nd to a neutral 2nd (see example 116). Had it not been for the lowering of the 5th above, the two

Example 116

intervals which are the centre of melodic activity in *Muye* (3rd to 4th, and 4th to 5th above) would have been completely different in *Segāh* and in *Čahārgāh*. In *Segāh* they are both neutral seconds, and in *Čahārgāh*, without the lowered 5th, they would be minor and major

2nds. But, with the lowering of the 5th above, the higher interval becomes a neutral 2nd. This results in a near approximation of the two modes of *Muye* in the two *dastgāh*s.

The melodic formula for *Muye* of *Čahārgāh* can be seen in example 117. An improvisation on it is seen in example 118 (p. 145).

Example 117

Hesār

With *Hesār*, a modulation to the 'key' of the 5th above is effected. The intervallic structure of the mode of *Čahārgāh* is retained, but the tones are applied rather differently. Above all, the tetrachord below the finalis is no longer the focal point of melodic formation; only the 2nd below maintains its prominent role.

The modal scheme in *Hesār* is given in example 119. The characteristics of this mode are:

Example 119

1. The range of the most emphasised tones in this mode is limited to a small third (f⁺ to aᵖ). This fact is a point of similarity between *Hesār* and *Muye* of *Čahārgāh*. But the three tones which are the centre of melodic activity are not the same in *Hesār* and *Muye*. In *Hesār* this small third is located a whole-tone higher.
2. The finalis has a central position in relation to other tones in the mode, just as the finalis has in the original mode of *Čahārgāh*.
3. The 2nd above is the *āqāz*, which with the finalis comprise the two tones dominating the melodic formation.
4. The 2nd below is next in prominence.
5. The 3rd below and the 3rd above are used less frequently.
6. The 4th above is rarely heard.
7. The *forud* pattern, as in the mode of *Čahārgāh*, concludes with a leap of a neutral 3rd, from the 3rd below to the finalis.
8. The melodic movement, except in the *forud* area, is overwhelmingly diatonic.

The modal similarities between *Hesār* of *Čahārgāh* and *Hesār* of *Segāh* are quite clear. They both require a key modulation to a perfect fifth above, and both concentrate on a limited melodic range, normally not exceeding the area from a third below to a third above their respective finalis.

The basic melodic formula for *Hesār* of *Čahārgāh* can be seen in example 120. As we can see, the similarity between this formula and the one given for *Hesār* of *Segāh* is quite striking (see example 100). An improvisation on this melodic formula is shown in example 121 (p. 146).

Example 120

Moxālef

It has been noted that in *Segāh*, *guše-ye Moxālef* presents a new modal structure where the 6th above the finalis of the mode of *Segāh* becomes the new finalis. In *Čahārgāh* the same process provides for the finalis for *Moxālef*. Yet, the modes of *Moxālef* of *Segāh* and the *Moxālef* of *Čahārgāh* are different. In *Čahārgāh*, the modal scheme for *Moxālef* is as given in example 122.

Example 122

The characteristics of this mode are:

1.   The finalis and *šāhed* are the same tone, which is the 6th above the finalis of *Čahārgāh*.
2.   The melodic activity centres around the 4th below to the 2nd above this finalis.
3.   The 4th below is the usual *āqāz*.
4.   The melodic movement is diatonic except for occasional leaps of thirds.

The basic melodic formula for *Moxālef* of *Čahārgāh* can be seen in example 123, and an improvisation on this melodic idea is given in example 124 (p. 146).

Example 123

In discussing the *Moxālef* of *Segāh*, we mentioned its modal similarity to that of *Bayāt-e Esfahān*. The mode of *Moxālef* of *Čahārgāh*, on the other hand, shows affinity with that of *Homāyun*. This is particularly true of their intervallic structure and their common *šāhed*. Chapter 11, which deals with *dastgāh-e Homāyun*, will clarify this similarity. It is interesting to note, also, that the modes of *Bayāt-e Esfahān* and *Homāyun* are traditionally considered to be related to one another.

Maqlub

As has been observed in the case of *dastgāh-e Segāh*, *guše-ye Maqlub* represents an extension of the mode established by the *Moxālef* to a higher register of sound. The emphasis here is on the tetrachord above the finalis, instead of the tetrachord below the finalis, which was the focal point of *Moxālef*. The mode of *Maqlub* will take on the form given in example 125. The characteristics of this mode are now somewhat different from the mode of *Moxālef* in *Segāh*.

Example 125

1. The finalis is usually the *āqāz*.
2. The 4th and the 3rd below have lost their significance.
3. The 2nd below is important as a 'leading tone' to the finalis; it also functions occasionally as the *āqāz*.
4. The 3rd above, after the finalis, is the most dominant tone.
5. The 4th above, absent in *Moxālef*, is now frequently used.

The basic melodic formula for *Maqlub* of *Čahārgāh* is given in example 126, and an improvisation on this skeletal idea is shown in example 127 (p. 146).

Example 126

Hodi

After *Maqlub*, which is in the area of *ōj*, and as such, is the climactic point in the *dastgāh*, *guše-ye Mansuri* may be performed, which is also in the same high register. However, if a more complete rendering of *dastgāh-e Čahārgāh* is under way, the three affiliated *gušes* of *Hodi*, *Pahlavi* and *Rajaz* are performed before *Mansuri*. These three *gušes* are traditionally considered to be 'heroic' pieces. In vocal improvisations, verses from the great epic cycle of the *Šāhnāme* by Ferdōsi are sung to melodies in the modes of these *gušes*.

Hodi, *Pahlavi*, and *Rajaz* are always performed in that order. As a group, they represent a separate entity, which makes them seem almost as one piece in an 'ABA form'. The first and last pieces of the three are very similar to one another, and employ tones up to the 7th above the finalis. The middle piece, on the other hand, is melodically distinct from the other two, and rises on to the area of the 8th and 9th above the finalis.

Since the finalis for all three of these *gušes* is the same as the original *Čahārgāh* finalis, a descent from the area of *Maqlub* to the area of *Hodi* becomes necessary. For a smooth transition to the lower octave, another improvisation in *Muye* is frequently inserted at this point. This provides a shift of emphasis to the area of the 4th and the 5th above the *Čahārgāh* finalis. But, as has been shown, the 5th above in *Muye* is lowered by a microtone (see example 116). A similar return to *Muye* was encountered in *dastgāh-e Segāh*, when a descent from *Maqlub* to the concluding piece of that *dastgāh* was to be achieved (see chapter 9).

After the improvisation in *Muye*, whose cadence falls on the original *Čahārgāh* finalis, *Hodi* is performed. *Hodi* employs the mode of *Čahārgāh* but extends it beyond the first tetrachord above, with no emphasis on the tetrachord below the finalis (see example 128). The nucleus of the *Hodi* melody is in two parts, as shown in example 129. After the (b) phrase the (a) phrase is

Example 128

Example 129

reintroduced; thus, by itself, *Hodi* also has an ABA design. An improvisation in *Hodi* is shown in example 130 (p. 147).

Pahlavi

In *Pahlavi* the above mode is changed slightly. At the very beginning of this *guše*, the 3rd above the finalis becomes the *āqāz*, and is lowered by a microtone (e$^{\natural}$ to e^{P}). The reason for this change seems to rest on the fact that the theme starts with a leap of a fourth up from the 3rd to the 6th above, and the fourth must always be a perfect interval. However, after the opening of the theme, the 3rd above is corrected to the original (e$^{\natural}$). Another peculiarity of *Pahlavi* is that it extends the mode up to the 9th above the finalis with emphasis on the tetrachord from the 5th to the 8th above. The modal scheme of *Pahlavi* is, therefore, as given in example 131. The basic formula for *Pahlavi* can be seen in example 132. Both the leap of a

Example 131

Example 132

fourth, from the 3rd to the 6th above, and the leap of a neutral third, from the 6th to the 8th above, are characteristic of the opening statement of *Pahlavi*, and, as such, give it a very distinctive melodic form. The unusually wide gamut of the melody is also distinctive of *Pahlavi*. An improvisation on this formula is shown in example 133 (p. 147).

Rajaz

Rajaz seems to be little more than a variation on the theme of *Hodi*. The same modal characteristics prevail. The theme is closely related to that of *Hodi*, and is also in two phrases. The basic formula is given in example 134, and an improvisation in *Rajaz* is shown in example 135 (p. 148).

Example 134

Mansuri

With *guše-ye Mansuri*, again the emphasis is shifted to the area of the 8th above. As such, we see that it would be logical for *Mansuri* to follow *Maqlub*. Indeed, if *Hodi*, *Pahlavi* and *Rajaz*, which are optional pieces, are omitted, *Mansuri* will follow *Maqlub*. However, its modal characteristics are not the same as *Maqlub*, as example 136 demonstrates.

Example 136

The characteristics of this mode are:

1.   It has a limited range of primarily three tones. It may be observed that the intervals between these three tones are the same as the intervals of the three notes emphasised in the mode of *Muye*. While the notes themselves are different, the intervals in both cases are minor and neutral seconds (see example 116, p. 58).
2.   The finalis is the 8th above the finalis of the *Čahārgāh* mode.
3.   The 2nd above the finalis is the *āqāz*.
4.   The 2nd below functions as *ist*.
5.   The 3rd and the 4th above, reached in the climactic portion of the improvisation, give us the highest tones used in the whole *dastgāh*.
6.   The 3rd and particularly the 4th below are non-essential tones.

The basic formula for *Mansuri* is shown in example 137, and an improvisation on the theme is shown in example 138 (p. 148).

Example 137

The conclusion of a performance of the *dastgāh* will be, as expected, in the original mode of *Čahārgāh*. After *Mansuri*, the emphasis is shifted back to the lower octave and an improvisation, much in the nature of a *darāmad*, is performed. Accordingly, the tetrachord below the finalis once again becomes the focal point. As noted in the case of *Segāh*, this extensive process of return, from a high register to the low register of the original mode of *Čahārgāh*, demonstrates the very nature and function of a *forud*.

11 Dastgāh-e Homāyun

One of the lengthiest of *dastgāh*s, *Homāyun* is also a very popular *dastgāh* among Persians. The modal scheme in *Homāyun* is as given in example 139. The bracketed tetrachord in this scale

Example 139

is virtually the same as the basic tetrachords in the modes of *Afšāri* and *Segāh*. But here, this tetrachord is employed in a completely different manner. It is such specific applications of tones in seemingly identical intervallic relationships which give individuality and meaning to Persian modes. To be sure, the tones that follow the tetrachord shown here do not create the same intervals as the follow-up tones in the modes of *Afšāri* and *Segāh*. This fact also emphasises the individuality of the mode of *Homāyun*, which indeed is never confused with, or thought to be related to, the other two.

The characteristics of the mode of *Homāyun* are the following:

1. It covers the range of a neutral seventh, from the 3rd below to the 5th above the finalis.
2. The area of the greatest melodic concentration is the tetrachord from the 3rd below to the 2nd above.
3. The 3rd below is the usual *āqāz*.
4. The 2nd below is the *ist*.
5. The 2nd above is the *šāhed*.
6. The 6th above is rarely used. When used, it is lower, by a microtone, than its lower octave (the 3rd below).

Forud

In its *forud*, the mode of *Homāyun* dwells on three tones from the 3rd below to the finalis. Typically, however, the concluding motif is the so-called *Bāl-e Kabutar* (pigeon's wing) which is used also in the modes of *Šur*, *Navā* and *Rāst*. In *Homāyun*, *Šur* and *Navā*, this motif makes use of the 4th above and the finalis in the manner shown in example 140.[1] A typical

Example 140

Example 141

forud pattern in the mode of *Homāyun* can be seen in example 141. The use of the *Bāl-e Kabutar* ending, however, is not mandatory, and the ending on the finalis can be simply approached from the 2nd below or the 2nd above, as shown in example 142.

Example 142

In *dastgāh-e Homāyun*, which contains numerous pieces not in the mode of *Homāyun* itself, the role of the *forud*, as a unifying agent, is particularly important. As shall be presently shown, most of the *gušes* of this *dastgāh* do not employ the modal scheme of the *darāmads*. Yet, the use of a standard *forud* at the conclusion of each *guše* helps to cement the group into a more logical whole.

*Darāmad*s

In the *darāmad* area the modal characteristics stated above are the main governing elements. The movement is overwhelmingly diatonic. A leap of a neutral 3rd, from the 2nd to the 4th above, is occasionally employed. The basic formula for the *darāmad*s of *Homāyun* is given in example 143, and an improvisation on this skeletal melodic idea is shown in example 144 (p. 149).

Example 143

In no other *dastgāh* do we find the initial modal structure, as represented by the *darāmad*s, to be as quickly abandoned as in *dastgāh-e Homāyun*. Immediately after the *darāmad*s, modulation to distinctly different modes are effected. But the forud pattern of the original mode, sometimes in a lengthy and highly embellished form, consistently intervenes to remind us of the mode of *Homāyun*. The important *gušes* of this *dastgāh* are the following: *Čahārgāh, Movāliān, Čakāvak, Abolčap, Tarz, Leyli-o Majnun, Bidād, Ney Dāvud, Nōruzhā, Nafir, Zābol, Bayāt-e Ajam, Ozzāl, Šuštari, Mansuri, Baxtiāri* and *Moālef*.

Čahārgāh

The use of a short *guše* by the name of *Čahārgāh* in *dastgāh-e Homāyun* is an example of the complexity of the *dastgāh* system, and can be a confusing matter. The fact is that the tetrachord above the finalis in the mode of *Homāyun* is identical with the same tetrachord in the mode of *Čahārgāh* (see chapter 10). The tetrachord below the finalis is different in the two modes. If, however, the 2nd below in the mode of *Homāyun* should be raised by a half-step, that tetrachord also becomes the same as in *Čahārgāh*. This alteration of the 2nd below and resultant modulation to *Čahārgāh* has become common practice in *dastgāh-e Homāyun*, at a point shortly after the *darāmad* area. Thus, the mode for this *guše* will be as shown in example 145. With the change of f to f, this simple modulation is achieved. The piece, which is

Example 145

improvised under the title of '*guše-ye Čahārgāh*', is very much in the nature of a *darāmad* of *Čahārgāh*, and concludes with a *Čahārgāh forud* (see chapter 10).

The melodic formula, here, is as given in example 146, and an improvisation on this theme

Example 146

is shown in example 147 (p. 149). This is not the only instance in *dastgāh-e Homāyun* where a modulation to *Čahārgāh* takes place. *Guše-ye Mansuri* is also in the mode of *Čahārgāh*, and shall be discussed later.

Movāliān

It has been shown that (as with the other *dastgāh*s) the mode of *Homāyun* and the musical examples are in the 'key' most commonly used on *tār* and *setār* in actual practice. In the case of the previously discussed *dastgāh*s, the finalis has been a relatively low pitch and the tendency has been to move up, gradually, to a higher register. In *Homāyun*, however, the most common finalis (g) is in the middle register and the gradual climb to higher registers would necessitate a sound level too high for the singer and the instrumentalist alike.[2]

In practice, after the *darāmad*s of *Homāyun*, and *guše-ye Čahārgāh*, the centre of activity is shifted, not up, but down to the lower octave. Thus the g, an octave below the original finalis, becomes the new finalis.

One may ask why this low g is not used as the finalis to begin with. The reason is that in the *darāmad* area of *Homāyun* there is considerable emphasis on the two tones immediately below the finalis, and these two tones, if the lower octave were used, are in an awkward register for such instruments as the *tār* and *setār*.[3] After the *darāmad* area, however, the two tones below the finalis lose their significance, except in *forud*, and the shift to the lower octave will create no problems.

This shift, to the g below middle c as the new finalis, is achieved by means of *Movāliān*, which is a transitional piece and always follows the last *darāmad* or the *guše-ye Čahārgāh* (if this *guše* is included in the performance). The 2nd below, which in *guše-ye Čahārgāh* was raised by a semi-tone, is lowered to its original form (f to f, in our scale). The 2nd above is raised by a microtone (a^p to a); it also loses its position as the *šāhed*. The 3rd below is lowered by a microtone; and as such it is no longer the 3rd below, but the 6th above (e^p to e^b). (Refer to the mode of *Homāyun*, example 139.)

After hovering briefly, *Movāliān* descends from the 'high' finalis to the area of the new 'low' finalis. In the course of this melodic transition, the 4th and the 5th above receive particular attention, which is a preview of a new trend that will be established by the *gušes* to come. Thus, *Movāliān* will cover the unusually wide range of a twelfth.

The basic melodic formula for *Movāliān* is given in example 148, and an improvisation is shown in example 149 (p. 150).

Example 148

Čakāvak

With *Čakāvak* the mode of *Homāyun* becomes somewhat transformed. The 2nd and the 3rd below lose their prominence as the *āqāz* and the *ist* respectively, and the centre of melodic activity is shifted higher, up to the 7th above. The modal scheme for *Čakāvak* can be seen in example 150. The characteristics of this mode are as follows:

Example 150

1.   The 4th above is the most prominent degree; it is the *šāhed*, as well as the usual *āqāz* and *ist*.
2.   Melodic formation concentrates on the pentachord above the finalis.
3.   The 2nd above is no longer emphasised.
4.   The 2nd and the 3rd below, contrary to the mode of *Homāyun* itself, are entirely non-essential.
5.   The 6th and the 7th above are used in the melodic climax.
6.   The melodic movement is overwhelmingly diatonic. The only permissible leaps are leaps of perfect fourths from the finalis to the 4th above, or from the 4th to the 7th above.

The basic melodic formula for *Čakāvak* is shown in example 151, and example 152 (p. 152) shows an improvisation on this melodic idea.

Example 151

Abolčap

Abolčap is in the mode of *Čakāvak*, with the same general characteristics but with its own distinct melodic idea. The basic formula for *Abolčap* can be seen in example 153. Example 154 (p. 150) is the transcription of an improvisation on this formula.

Example 153

Tarz

This *guše* is also in the mode of *Čakāvak* and does not present any individual modal characteristics. Its basic formula can be seen in example 155, and an improvisation on it in example 156 (p. 151).

Example 155

Leyli-o Majnun

This is also in the mode of *Čakāvak*, and appears to be a variant of the same basic melodic idea on which all of these *gušes* (*Čakāvak*, *Abolčap* and *Tarz*) are founded.

The basic melodic formula for *Leyli-o Majnun* is given in example 157. Example 158 (p. 151) is an improvisation on this melodic idea.

Example 157

Bidād

Guše-ye Bidād extends the mode of *Čakāvak* to a still higher register, up to the 9th above the finalis. Also, the 5th above assumes greater prominence than before to the extent of becoming the *šahed*. *Bidād*'s modal scheme is given in example 159. The characteristics of this mode are the following:

Example 159

1.   The melodic activity centres around the area of the 3rd to the 8th above the finalis.
2.   The finalis and the 2nd above are used only in the *forud*.
3.   The 3rd above is the *āqāz*.
4.   The 4th above is the *ist*.
5.   The 5th above is the *šāhed*.
6.   The 9th above is used in the climactic area of the melodic improvisation and is flatter than its lower octave by a microtone (a^+ instead of a^p).
7.   The melodic movement is basically step-wise; occasional leaps of 3rds among the tones of the tetrachord above the 4th are used.

The basic melodic pattern for *Bidād* can be seen in example 160, and an improvisation on this skeletal idea would be as shown in example 161 (p. 151).

Example 160

Ney Dāvud

Guše-ye Ney Dāvud is very similar to *Bidād*; in fact, it may be regarded as a mere variant of the theme of *Bidād*. Its mode and character are entirely the same as those of *Bidād*. Example 162 shows the basic thematic idea for *Ney Dāvud*, and an improvisation on this idea is represented by example 163 (p. 152).

Example 162

Nōruzhā

There are three related *gušes* which go under the names of *Nōruz-e Arab*, *Nōruz-e Sabā*, and *Nōruz-e Xārā*. Their musical similarity to one another is even more striking than that of their titles. They shall be considered here, collectively, as one *guše*. In their modal structure, they present somewhat new elements which are shared by *Nafir*, a *guše* which usually follows the *Nōruzhā*. The most significant change in this new mode is that a finalis other than that of

Example 164

Homāyun is presented. Example 164 shows a modal scheme for the *Nōruzhā*. The characteristics of this mode are:

1. Melodic activity concentrates around the 2nd below to the 3rd above the finalis.
2. The 2nd below is the usual *āqāz*.
3. The 3rd above is occasionally raised by a microtone (e^b to e^p) in an ascending movement. Although this change is rare and is not used with marked consistency, it is sufficiently elemental in this mode to be recognised as a *moteqayyer*. This change of e^b to e^p is not the same as the use of e^p as the 3rd below and e^b s the 6th above, in the mode of *Homāyun*. Here, they are both variants of the 3rd above the finalis of the mode.
4. The melodic movement is largely step-wise; leaps are restricted to thirds, except in cadences where the *Bāl-e Kabutar* motif is used (see example 140).
5. There are no distinct *forud* patterns, except for the *Bāl-e Kabutar* ending.
6. Apart from having a *moteqayyer*, this mode is very close to the mode of *Bayāt-e Esfahān*, which will be covered in the next chapter.

The basic melodic formula for *Nōruzhā* is given in example 165, and an improvisation on this idea is shown in example 166 (p. 153). This is a transcription of *Nōruz-e Xārā*.

Example 165

Nafir

This *guše* is in the same mode as that of the *Nōruzhā*, but moves up to the area of the 6th above the finalis. The 5th above receives particular emphasis. The use of the raised 3rd degree (e^p) is more prominent and consistent in *Nafir* than in *Nōruzhā*. Example 167 shows the basic melodic formula for *Nafir*. Example 168 (p. 153) represents the transcription of an improvisation on this melodic idea.

Example 167

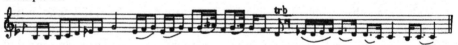

Zābol

It has been observed in chapters 9 and 10 that *guše-ye Zābol* is an important *guše* of *dastgāh-e Segāh* and *Čahārgāh*. It is also performed here but it comes to *Homāyun* from *Segāh* and not from *Čahārgāh*. This seems rather curious since, as already shown, there is a clear affinity between the modes of *Homāyun* and *Čahārgāh*, but not with *Segāh*. However, this anomaly is explained by the fact that *Zābol* in *dastgāh-e Homāyun* is performed after *Bidād* or after *Nōruzhā*, and in both cases the first tetrachord of the mode of *Homāyun*, which is identical with the first tetrachord of the mode of *Čahārgāh*, is not emphasised. The focal points are the 4th and 5th above, and in this area there is no affinity with *Čahārgāh*.

On the other hand, in raising the 6th above the finalis of *Homāyun* by a microtone (e^b to e^p) the mode of *Zābol* of *Segāh* is easily obtained. *Zābol* of *Homāyun* is based on the modal scheme given in example 169. We notice that the tetrachord of *Zābol* is virtually the same as the main tetrachord of *Homāyun* itself (example 139), except that the tones of the two tetrachords do

Example 169

not have identical functions. The finalis and the *āqāz* of *Zābol* is only the *āqāz* in *Homāyun*, and the finalis of *Homāyun* is the *šāhed* of *Zābol*.

For musical examples of *Zābol*, see chapter 9.

Bayāt-e Ajam

In *dastgāh-e Homāyun*, *Zābol* is usually followed by *guše-ye Bayāt-e Ajam*, which is, in spite of its important sounding title,[4] simply a variation on the theme of *Zābol*. If both *Zābol* and *Bayāt-e Ajam* are performed, the former concludes with a *Segāh forud*, but the latter modulates back to the mode of *Homāyun* and uses a *Homāyun forud*.

Since *Zābol* has been discussed in connection with *dastgāh-e Segāh* (chapter 9), and musical examples for this *guše* have been given, an example of an improvisation in *Bayāt-e Ajam* with its conclusion in the mode of *Homāyun*, is provided here. Its basic melodic formula is very similar to that of *Zābol*, and is shown in example 170. A transcription of an improvisation in *Bayāt-e Ajam* is given in example 171 (p. 154).

Example 170

Ozzāl

With *Ozzāl*, another common modulation in *dastgāh-e Homāyun*, this time to the mode of *Šur*, is effected. As in *dastgāh-e Šur*, *Ozzāl* is performed in the area of the *ōj*. In the *Homāyun* of the 'key' of g, which is the basis of the transcriptions here, the *ōj* would mean a return to the higher register in which the *darāmad*s have been presented. The only change of pitch required for the modal transition from *Homāyun* to *Šur*, therefore, will be a lowering of the 3rd above by a semi-tone (b to bᵇ). The modal scheme for *Ozzāl* can be seen in example 172. For musical examples of the melodic formula and an improvisation in *Ozzāl*, see chapter 4.

Example 172

Šuštari

Guše-ye Šuštari is one of the most important of the *guše*s of *dastgāh-e Homāyun*. With *Mansuri* and *Baxtiāri*, they constitute the climactic conclusion of the *dastgāh*. All three are in the area of *ōj*. The mode of *Šuštari* is essentially that of *Homāyun*, but the 2nd and the 3rd below the

Example 173

finalis have no role of any significance. The range of melody in *Šuštari* is higher than in *Homāyun* itself, and extends up to the 7th above. *Šuštari*'s modal scheme is given in example 173. The characteristics of this mode are:

1. The 2nd above is not the *šahed* as in the mode of *Homāyun*, but is the *ist*.
2. The 4th above is the *šahed*.
3. After the *šahed*, all of the tones of the pentachord above the finalis are used with near equal emphasis.
4. The movement is essentially stepwise. One characteristic leap of a fourth is used in the highest point of the improvisation from the 4th to the 7th above.

The basic melodic formula for *Šuštari* is shown in example 174, and an improvisation on the theme is given in example 175 (p. 154).

Example 174

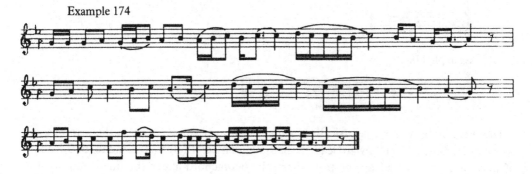

Mansuri

With *guše-ye Mansuri*, the affinity between *Homāyun* and *Čahārgāh* is established once more. *Mansuri* is, in fact, rightly from the repertory of *Čahārgāh*. Here, however, the 4th above the finalis of *Homāyun* becomes the new finalis, whereas in *guše-ye Čahārgāh*, performed shortly after the *darāmad*s of *Homāyun*, the finalis was the same as that of *Homāyun*. The reason for the change of finalis here is that by moving to the 4th above the finalis of *Homāyun* a higher register of sound is exploited, which is in keeping with the tradition of heightening tension near the end of the performance of a *dastgāh*. Furthermore, in *Šuštari*, the 4th above has been the *šahed*, and the shift to that tone as the new finalis creates no jolt or surprise.

Example 176 shows the modal scheme of *Mansuri*. The mode, as well as the tone functions,

Example 176

are identical with those of *Mansuri* as discussed in *Čahārgāh* (chapter 10). In order to modulate to *Mansuri*, two modifications in the mode of *Šuštari* have become necessary: the 5th above is lowered by a microtone (d to dᵖ); and the 6th above is raised by a semi-tone (eᵇ to e). For musical examples of *Mansuri* see chapter 10.

Baxtiāri

Guše-ye Baxtiāri takes us back in the realm of *Homāyun* proper. Yet, *Baxtiāri* seems to combine modal characteristics of *Šuštari* with those of *Homāyun*. As in *Šuštari*, the main area of concentration is the pentachord above the finalis, and the *āqāz* is the same note as the finalis. But there is no *ist* other than the finalis itself, and there is no definite *šahed*. At the same time, as in the mode of *Homāyun*, the 2nd and the 3rd below the finalis have a degree of importance. They are heard in a typical *Baxtiāri* phrase-ending which concludes with the motif, or a variant of it, given in example 177. The modal scheme for *Baxtiāri* is shown in example 178.

Example 177

Example 178

The melodic movement is basically diatonic. However, in addition to the leap of a 4th shown in example 177, an upward leap of a half-augmented 4th, from the 2nd to the 5th above (aᵖ to d, and downward leaps of 3rds within the pentachord above the finalis, are used in *Baxtiāri*.

Example 179 shows the basic melodic formula for *Baxtiāri* and an improvisation on it is shown in example 180 (p. 155).

Example 179

Moālef

Moālef is a small but striking *guše* which is usually performed before the final *forud* in *dastgāh-e Homāyun*. It is an interesting piece as it represents one of the few instances in Persian music when a microtone is used as a melodic interval, and, at least in performances on *tār* and *setār*, seems to be a fixed aspect of *Moālef*.

This microtone is achieved by lowering the 3rd above by a whole-tone (b to bᵇᵇ). This bᵇᵇ is

Example 181

used as an ornamental neighbouring tone – almost in the nature of a grace note which follows rather than precedes the main note – to the 2nd above. Except for this peculiarity, the mode of *Moālef* is the same as the mode of *Baxtiāri*, as can be seen in example 181. The basic melodic formula for *Moālef* is given in example 182, and a transcription of an extended improvisation on this melodic idea is given in example 183 (p. 155).

Example 182

After *Moālef*, or after *Baxtiāri* if *Moālef* has been omitted, the performer will re-establish the mode of *Homāyun* by concluding with an extensive *forud*. This extended *forud* is all the more necessary since, as we have seen, *Homāyun* can be a lengthy and varied *dastgāh* in which there is considerable flexibility in the order of *gušes*, and in the use of low, middle and high registers of sound. The convenient orderliness noticed in other *dastgāh*s discussed so far, particularly in *Segāh* and *Čahārgāh*, is not present in the structure of *Homāyun*. Therefore, a lengthy *forud* improvisation is important in establishing a sense of cohesion before the *dastgāh* is brought to an end.

12 *Dastgāh-e Bayāt-e Esfahān*

Persian musicians commonly consider *Bayāt-e Esfahān* to be a derivative of *dastgāh-e Homāyun*. The argument is that if we begin on the 4th degree above the finalis of *Homāyun*, we shall achieve the mode of *Bayāt-e Esfahān*.[1] This argument may be, at best, as valid as to say that if we start from the 2nd degree of the Dorian mode we shall have the Phrygian mode, and that, therefore, the Phrygian is a derivative of the Dorian mode.

In fact, we have seen that Persian modes depend on much more than the mere similarities between intervals. When we consider all factors that contribute to the identity of a mode in Persian music, we are compelled to consider *Bayāt-e Esfahān* as an independent mode.

Aside from the argument stated above, there is one basis for confusing *Bayāt-e Esfahān* with *Homāyun*. In the latter *dastgāh*, those pieces which are in the mode of *Čahārgāh* do exhibit a marked similarity of characteristics with *Bayāt-e Esfahān*. It is possible, then, to confuse *Bayāt-e Esfahān* with the *Čahārgāh* area of *dastgāh-e Homāyun*. Of course, this similarity is limited to the modal characteristics; the melodic bases for *Bayāt-e Esfahān* and *Čahārgāh* are each sufficiently distinct not to be confused with one another.

Bayāt-e Esfahān is also considered to be the Persian counterpart of the harmonic minor mode of western music.[2] If we construct a scale of *Bayāt-e Esfahān* covering the range of an octave, all of its tones will correspond with the harmonic minor scale, except the 6th degree, which is higher by a microtone. But, again, we must point out that a scale, as such, is practically meaningless in Persian music, and that Persian modes depend on much more than just a certain arrangement of tones. Also the 6th degree, or the 3rd degree below the finalis, which is higher in *Bayāt-e Esfahān*, cannot easily be ignored, for it is the tone of *ist* and, as such, a very significant degree of the scale.

Example 184

Example 184 shows the modal scheme for *Bayāt-e Esfahān*. The characteristics of this mode are:

1. Most of the melodic activity concentrates on the area between the 4th below and the 3rd above the finalis.
2. The finalis is also the *šāhed* and the most common *āqāz*; the 4th below may also act as the *āqāz*.
3. The 3rd below is the *ist*. It is likely that not only phrases but also a whole piece would end on that degree instead of the finalis.
4. The tetrachord above the finalis is the minor tetrachord. Occasionally, when that area of the mode is emphasised, the similarity to the minor mode of western music is noticed.

5.   The melodic movement is overwhelmingly diatonic.

6.   In recent decades, under the influence of western music, a growing tendency to raise the 2nd below, to create a genuine 'leading tone' feeling, has resulted in what is called the 'modern' mode of *Bayāt-e Esfahān*. In this new mode, the f$^{\sharp}$ of the above scale becomes f$^{\natural}$, and a greater affinity with the scale of the harmonic minor is achieved. Perhaps this is comforting to some, but here we shall stay with the authentic form of this mode.

It should be added that the argument which is presented to establish *Bayāt-e Esfahān* as a derivative of *Homāyun* can only be in respect of the 'modern' mode of *Esfahān*. Also, by starting on the 4th degree of the mode of *Homāyun* and continuing to its higher octave, we do not achieve the traditional but the modern mode of *Bayāt-e Esfahān* (see example 185).

Example 185

Another reason for considering *Bayāt-e Esfahān* to be independent of *Homāyun* is that it does not employ the *foruds* of *Homāyun*, but has its own *forud* patterns. *Bayāt-e Esfahān* does not use the *Bāl-e Kabutar* motif; the approach to the finalis is customarily from below, by way of the 2nd, or 3rd and the 2nd below, to the finalis. A typical *forud* in *Bayāt-e Esfahān* would be as given in example 186.

Example 186

Since ending a phrase, or even a piece, on the *ist* instead of the finalis is very common, the *forud* pattern for this type of ending must also be discussed. A peculiarity of this type of ending is a trill on the 2nd below (f$^{\sharp}$). This trill stylistically is not from f$^{\sharp}$ to g but to g$^{\flat}$, which results in a microtonal trill. Needless to say, that g, which is actually the finalis of our mode, is not lowered in any other situation; and here g$^{\flat}$ is used purely as an optional ornamentation.

Example 187 is a *forud* of *Bayāt-e Esfahān* ending on the *ist*.

Example 187

Darāmads

In the case of a large *dastgāh*, such as *Homāyun* or *Čahārgāh*, we have seen that the basic mode of that *dastgāh* is effective in the *darāmad* area which is but a small part of the whole *dastgāh*. In smaller *dastgāhs*, such as *Bayāt-e Tork* and now *Bayāt-e Esfahān*, the *darāmad* section is proportionately a large part of the whole and the basic mode is also proportionately maintained for a longer period.

The *darāmad* of *Bayāt-e Esfahān*, which represent the modal characteristics discussed above, are based on the following melodic formula given in example 188. Example 189 (p. 156) is an improvisation on the thematic idea of the *darāmad* in *Bayāt-e Esfahān*.

Example 188

Dastgāh-e Bayāt-e Esfahān does not contain a large body of pieces. Its main *gušes* are *Jāmedarān*, *Bayāt-e Rāje'*, *Oššāq*, *Šāhxatāi* and *Suz-o Godāz*. Of these, *Jāmedarān* will be discussed as one of the *tekke*s in chapter 16, and *Oššāq* has already been covered in chapter 6, on *dastgāh-e Dašti*.

Bayāt-e Rāje'

After the *darāmad*s, *Bayāt-e Rāje'* constitutes the most important part of *dastgāh-e Bayāt-e Esfahān*. While fundamentally an extension of the mode of *Esfahān*, the mode of *Bayāt-e*

Example 190

Rāje' is sufficiently different to be seen as a new modal scheme (see example 190). The characteristics of this mode and its relationship with that of *Bayāt-e Esfahān* are as follows:

1.   The finalis is the same as that of *Bayāt-e Esfahān*, but it has less prominence in the course of melodic improvisations.
2.   The 2nd above is the most important tone. It is the *šāhed*, the *ist*, and the usual *āqāz*.
3.   The centre of melodic activity is the pentachord above the finalis.
4.   The tetrachord below the finalis, in contrast to *Bayāt-e Esfahān*, is no longer emphasised, and, except for the 2nd below, can be omitted altogether.

Example 191 gives the basic melodic formula for *Bayāt-e Rāje'*, and example 192 (p. 157) is the transcription of an improvisation on this idea.

Example 191

Oššāq

After *Bayāt-e Rāje' guše-ye Oššāq* is usually performed. This *guše* has been discussed in chapter 6. The *Oššāq* of *Bayāt-e Esfahān* is another improvisation on the melodic basis given there. In *Bayāt-e Esfahān*, the mode of *Oššāq* is constructed on the 2nd degree of the *Esfahān* mode as its finalis. Accordingly, the third above the finalis of *Esfahān* is raised by a microtone (b♭ to b^p) and the 7th above (and the 2nd below, which is seldom used) is lowered by a microtone (f♯ to f¹). The modal scheme, therefore, is as shown in example 193. For musical examples of *Oššāq*, see chapter 6.

Example 193

Šāhxatāi

Šāhxatāi is another *guše* which is in a mode close to that of *Oššāq*, and very similar to that of *Šur*. This *guše* is commonly performed both in *Bayāt-e Esfahān* and in *dastgāh-e Navā*. The finalis of *Šāhxatāi* is the same as that of *Oššāq*. The *moteqayyer*, here, as in *Šur*, is the 5th above. This degree is normally a perfect fifth from the finalis, except occasionally in descending patterns when it is lowered by a microtone (e to e^p). Example 194 shows the modal scheme for *Šāhxatāi*.

Example 194

Šāhxatāi is a *guše* which constitutes the *ōj* in *Bayāt-e Esfahān*. As the scale in example 194 shows, it reaches the highest normal range used in the traditional music. Characteristic of its melody is a leap of a fourth at the beginning, from the 2nd below to the 3rd above the finalis. The basic melodic formula for *Šāhxatāi* is given in example 195. Example 196 (p. 157) shows an improvisation in *Šāhxatāi*.

Example 195

Whereas *Oššāq* may lead into *Šāhxatāi* without an *Esfahān forud*, *Šāhxatāi* must conclude with a modulation to *Bayāt-e Esfahān* and with an *Esfahān forud* (as shown in example 196), since the pieces which follow are again in the mode of *Bayāt-e Esfahān*.

Suz-o Godāz

The only distinctive *guše* in the repertoire of *Bayāt-e Esfahān*, which is performed after *Šāhxatāi*, is *Suz-o Godāz*. Its mode is an extension of that of *Bayāt-e Esfahān* itself, but with greater emphasis on the pentachord above the finalis. Example 197 shows the basic melodic

Example 197

formula for *Suz-o Godāz* and example 198 (p. 158) is the transcription of an improvisation on this idea.

In a vocal performance of *dastgāh-e Bayāt-e Esfahān*, it is traditional at this point for a *Masnavi* to be sung. *Masnavi* will be discussed in chapter 16. This *guše* can be sung in any of the twelve *dastgāh*s, but it is particularly common to *Afšāri* and to *Bayāt-e Esfahān*.

13 Dastgāh-e Navā

Dastgāh-e Navā and *Dastgāh-e Rast-Panjgāh* are the two least performed of Persian *dastgāh*s. There are not many musicians who know all the *guše*s of these two *dastgāh*s. It is difficult to find a reason why *Navā* is not more commonly performed. While it contains a number of pieces which are performed in one or more of the other *dastgāh*s, it does embody a number of *guše*s peculiar to its own repertoire. *Rāst-Panjgāh*'s lack of popularity, on the other hand, is due to more tangible reasons which will be discussed in chapter 15.

Traditionally, *Navā* is regarded as one of the seven *dastgāh*s. But, among twentieth-century Persian musicians, Ali Naqi Vaziri and his disciple, Ruhollāh Xāleqi, have considered *Navā* as a derivative of *dastgāh-e Šur*.[1] Their view is a personal one, based mostly on the fact that the scale of *Navā* can be constructed from the 4th degree of the scale of *Šur*. This is the same sort of argument which is given to establish *Bayāt-e Esfahān* as a derivative of *Homāyun*, considered and rejected in the preceding chapter. Again, it must be emphasised that the very notion of scales is quite irrelevant to Persian music. Persian modes are conceived around a few notes, often not exceeding a tetrachord. Above all, it is the role of these tones and their relationships to one another that determine the identity of the modes. Their arrangements into octave scales has led to undue attention to such scales and has placed significance where there is none. To suggest that if we were to start on this or that degree of this mode we will end up with this or that mode, and therefore the two are related, is false in western music, but in Persian music it is no less than ridiculous.

Example 199

Example 199 gives the modal scheme of *Navā*. The characteristics of this mode are:

1.   The finalis has a central position in relation to the area of melodic activity, which emphasises both the tetrachords below and above the finalis, but the former is favoured.
2.   The most common *āqāz* is the 2nd below, but the finalis itself and the 4th below also may function as the *āqāz*.
3.   The 3rd below is the *ist*. This is a point of similarity between the modes of *Navā* and *Bayāt-e Esfahān* (see chapter 12).

Another point of similarity between the modes of *Bayāt-e Esfahān* and *Navā* is that except for the 2nd below the finalis, the tones of the two modes are identical, and they function in a like manner. Also, when we consider the *guše*s of *Navā*, we find that, while they are more numerous, they include all of the *guše*s which are normally performed in *Bayāt-e Esfahān*. Can it be established, therefore, that these two *dastgāh*s are somehow related? There are no existing theories to this effect; and although a modulation from *Navā* to *Bayāt-e Esfahān*, or vice versa, can be accomplished very easily it is not done. The relationship of the two is, therefore, to some extent comparable to the relationship between *Segāh* and *Čahārgāh*.

Forud

Dastgāh-e Navā contains numerous *guše*s which are not in the mode of *Navā* itself. The use of a distinctive *forud* pattern is therefore essential for maintaining unity throughout the *dastgāh*. The most characteristic *forud* pattern is a long phrase which emphasises the finalis, as well as the 2nd and the 3rd below the finalis. It ends with the *Bāl-e Kabutar* motif (see chapter 11, example 140). A typical *Navā forud* is shown in example 200.

Example 200

Darāmads

In the *darāmad* area of *Navā*, the tetrachord below the finalis receives the greatest emphasis. The 2nd above the finalis is also frequently heard, but the 3rd and the 4th above are rarely reached. As is the case with every *dastgāh*, here the *darāmad*s are the most representative of the mode of *Navā*. The basic melodic formula for the *darāmad*s of *Navā* is given in example 201; an improvisation on this thematic idea is given in example 202 (p. 158).

Example 201

   Dastgāh-e Navā is not a very popular *dastgāh*. It is seldom performed and, when heard, it is often in an abbreviated form. The probable reason is that many of its *guše*s are not known to most musicians. In the present study, all of the more distinctive *guše*s of this *dastgāh* are considered, even though some of them may not be included in an ordinary '*majlesi*' (suited to a casual gathering) performance.

   The *guše*s of *dastgāh-e Navā* are *Gardāniye*, *Bayāt-e Rāje'*, *Nahoft*, *Gavešt*, *Neyšāburak*, *Xojaste*, *Arāq*, *Oššāq*, *Hoseyni*, *Busalik*, *Neyriz*, *Rahāvi*, *Nāqus* and *Taxt-e Tāqdis*.

Gardāniye

Gardāniye is a short *guše*; it is in the mode of *Navā*, and presents no new modal characteristics, except for the 3rd above which receives more attention than in the *darāmad*s, it is also the *āqāz* in *Gardāniye*. The basic formula for *Gardāniye* is shown in example 203. Example 204 (p. 159) is the transcription of an improvisation in *Gardāniye*.

Example 203

Bayāt-e Rāje'

We have discussed *Bayāt-e Rāje'* in chapter 12 on *Bayāt-e Esfahān*. It was shown there that the *Bayāt-e Rāje'* melody concentrates on the pentachord above the finalis. Since the pentachord above the finalis of *Navā* is identical with the same pentachord in *Bayāt-e Esfahān*, this *guše* can be performed in *Navā* without any alterations. Only when the *forud* is played do we find that we are, in fact, in *dastgāh-e Navā* and not in *Bayāt-e Esfahān*.

For musical examples of *Bayāt-e Rāje'*, see chapter 12.

Nahoft

For *guše-ye Nahoft*, the finalis is shifted one octave lower. As regards the musical shift to the lower octave, observations made about a similar move in *dastgāh-e Homāyun* hold true here (p. 67). In relation to this lower octave finalis, the 4th and 5th above become centres of melodic emphasis. The tetrachord below the finalis, which was of much importance in the

Example 205

*darāmad*s, is no longer heard except in the *forud*. Example 205 shows the modal scheme for *Nahoft*. The characteristics of this mode are:

1. The finalis does not play an important role except in the *forud*.
2. The 2nd above the finalis is the *ist*. In instrumental music, this note, when appearing as the *ist*, is often played with a trill. This is one of the few instances when Persian music provides for a prescribed ornamentation on a tone. Normally, the use of ornamentation, such as a trill, is left to the choice of the performer.
3. The 3rd and the 7th above are the least emphasised tones.
4. The 4th above is, after the 5th, the most commonly heard tone.
5. The 5th above is the dominating tone, and is therefore the *šāhed*. It is also the *āqāz*.
6. The 6th above is flatter than its lower octave (the 3rd below) by a microtone (e$^{\flat}$ instead of e^{P}). This sort of lowering of non-essential tones in the higher octave is common to most Persian modes, and has been already discussed on a number of previous occasions.

Example 206 gives the basic melodic formula for *Nahoft*, and example 207 shows an improvisation on this theme (p. 160).

Example 206

Gavešt

With *Gavešt*, a more striking change of mode takes place. The 2nd above the finalis of the mode of *Navā* is lowered by a microtone (a to a^p), and at the same time becomes the *šāhed*. The 5th above is also lowered by a microtone (d to d^p), but this degree has, now, only a negligible role. The 2nd below acts as the *ist*. Accordingly, this *guše* has a certain modal similarity to both *Afšāri* and *Segāh*.[2] The modal scheme for *Gavešt* is shown in example 208.

Example 208

A finalis for *Gavešt*, other than that of *Navā*, has not been recognised. The reason is that, in spite of its modal individuality, *Gavešt* is a short *guše* and soon yields to the mode of *Navā*.

Example 209 shows the basic melodic formula for *Gavešt*. The ornamental lowering of the

Example 209

4th above (c to c^b) is a point of distinct similarity to the mode of *Afšāri* (see chapter 8). It must be emphasised that this alteration, and the resultant chromaticism, is purely ornamental and can be omitted altogether.

Example 210 (p. 160) shows an improvisation on the theme of *Gavešt* and also demonstrates the modulation to the mode of *Navā*.

Neyšāburak

This *guše* brings us back to the area of *Navā*, but with emphasis on the 3rd and the 4th above the finalis. A characteristic of *Neyšāburak* is the leap of a perfect fourth from the finalis to the 4th above, shortly after the start of the melody. Its basic melodic formula can be seen in example 211, and example 212 (p. 161) shows an improvisation on this skeletal idea.

Example 211

Xojaste

With *Xojaste*, the focal point of the mode of *Navā* is raised higher to the area of the 5th and 6th above the finalis, both of which receive much emphasis. The 5th also acts as the *ist*. The 7th above is also heard much more than ever before. The finalis and the 2nd above are heard primarily in the *forud*. The modal scheme for *Xojaste* is therefore as shown in example 213a. Example 213b gives the basic formula for *Xojaste*, and a transcription of an improvisation can be seen in example 214 (p. 161).

Example 213a

Example 213b

Arāq

In discussing *guše-ye Nahib* in *dastgāh-e Afšāri* (chapter 8), it was mentioned that *Nahib*, *Arāq* and a number of other pieces comprise a distinct unit, presenting their own modal and melodic identity. This group of *guše*s are performed regularly in three of the twelve *dastgāh*s: *Māhur*, *Rāst* and *Navā*. They are more commonly identified with *Māhur*, however, and will therefore be discussed in chapter 14 on *dastgāh-e Māhur*.

Oššāq

Guše-ye Oššāq has been discussed in chapter 6, in connection with *dastgāh-e Dašti*. When performed in *dastgāh-e Navā*, its modal and melodic characteristics remain unchanged. The 4th below the finalis of *Navā* becomes the finalis for *Oššāq*. Accordingly, its modal scheme is as shown in example 215. For musical examples of *Oššāq*, see chapter 6.

Example 215

Hoseyni

Hoseyni is a *guše* from the repertoire of *dastgāh-e Šur*. Its mode and melodic make-up are the same as that given in *Šur*. Accordingly, the 4th below the finalis of *Navā*, which had become the finalis in *Oššāq*, retains that role, both here and in the remaining *guše*s of *dastgāh-e Navā*. In fact, after *Nahoft*, the modal dominance of *Navā* begins to lose ground. Yet the use of a *Navā forud* at the conclusion of each *guše* reminds the listener of the original mode of the *dastgāh*. With *Hoseyni*, however, a modulation to the mode of *Šur* is effected, and in the contemporary tradition, the *forud* of *Navā* is no longer used at its conclusion. Thus, all of the last *guše*s performed in *dastgāh-e Navā* appear to be in the realm of *Šur*. For the conclusion of each of these *guše*s, a *forud* of *Šur* is used and not one of *Navā*.

We have observed a similar occurrence in *dastgāh-e Afšāri*. No doubt in both *Afšāri* and *Navā*, the unhampered take-over of the mode of *Šur* has been responsible for the fact that they are regarded, by some, to be derivatives of *dastgāh-e Šur*. This belief is, of course, much more widely accepted in the case of *Afšāri* than for *Navā*. However, we see no reason why the original modes or characteristics of *Afšāri* or *Navā*, which are quite distinct, should be confused with those of *Šur*, even though in current practice the modulation to the mode of *Šur* and the dominance of that mode in the second half of both *Afšāri* and *Navā* cannot be denied.

For musical examples of *Hoseyni*, see chapter 4.

Busalik

Guše-ye Busalik also is based on the mode of *Šur*. Unlike *Hoseyni*, it is not played in *dastgāh-e Šur*, and is only performed in *dastgāh-e Navā*. Thus, we have another of those paradoxical situations (such as with *Oššāq*) where a *guše* is not performed in the *dastgāh* to whose mode it adheres, but is played in another *dastgāh*, where the initial mode is markedly different.

Busalik, however, makes use of a wider range than most *gušes* that are in the mode of *Šur*. The 4th above the finalis of *Šur* is the *šāhed*, and the 5th above is the *āqāz* in *Busalik*. There is no *moteqayyer*. The modal scheme for *Busalik* is given in example 216. The basic melodic

Example 216

formula for *Busalik* can be seen in example 217, and example 218 (p. 162) shows an improvisation on this theme (notice the *Šur forud* at the end of the *guše*).

Example 217

Neyriz

Guše-ye Neyriz is also in the realm of *Šur*. It is not performed in *dastgāh-e Šur*, however, but in *Navā*, *Māhur* and *Rāst-Panjgāh*.

In *Neyriz*, the emphasis is on the finalis and particularly on the 2nd above, which is the *šāhed*. The melodic activity centres around that tone, seldom going as high as the 4th above. The 2nd and 3rd below the finalis are heard very frequently, and the 3rd below is the *āqāz*. The modal scheme for *Neyriz* is, therefore, as shown in example 219. Example 220 gives the

Example 219

Example 220

basic melodic formula for *Neyriz* and example 221 shows an improvisation on this melodic idea (p. 163).

Rahāvi

Rahāvi emphasises the pentachord above the finalis of *Šur*. No one tone emerges as the *šāhed*; the 2nd below the finalis is the *āqāz*. Melodically, it is very sequential, with a leap of a perfect fourth, from the 2nd below to the 3rd above, as the distinguishing mark of its opening phrase.

Example 222 shows the basic formula for *Rahāvi*, while example 223 (p. 163) is the transcription of an improvisation in *Rahāvi*.

Example 222

Nāqus

In *guše-ye Nāqus*, the pentachord above the finalis of *Šur* is the focal point of melodic activity. The 5th above the finalis is the *šāhed*, the 3rd above the *āqāz*, and the 2nd below the *ist*. Its modal scheme, accordingly, is as given in example 224. The basic melodic formula for *Nāqus*

Example 224

can be seen in example 225, and an improvisation on this idea is shown in example 226 (p. 164).

Example 225

Taxt-e Tāqdis

In *guše-ye Taxt-e Tāqdis*, a wider range of the mode of *Šur* is employed. The 2nd below the finalis is the *āqāz*, as well as the *ist*. The *moteqayyer* of *Šur* – the 5th above the finalis lowered by a microtone – which was not used in any of the preceding *guše*s, is used at one point at the beginning of *Taxt-e Tāqdis'* melodic formula. Its modal scheme is demonstrated in example 227.

Example 227

As in *Rahāvi*, the *Taxt-e Tāqdis* melody begins with a leap of a fourth, from the 2nd below to the 3rd above. Example 228 gives its basic melodic formula, and an improvisation on this theme is shown in example 229 (p. 164).

Example 228

Thus, the last *guše* in *dastgāh-e Navā* is not in the mode of *Navā* but in the mode of *Śur*. On the other hand, it is possible to modulate, at the end of *Taxt-e Tāqdis*, back to the mode of *Navā* and conclude with a *forud* of *Navā*. Some contemporary musicians who are more conscious of the desirability of concluding in the original mode of the *dastgāh*, do, in fact, modulate back to *Navā*. This can be done simply by starting the *forud* pattern on the finalis of *Navā*, and performing a lengthy improvisation on the *forud* pattern (see the *forud* of *Navā*, example 200). Nevertheless, the dependence of *Navā*, not as a mode, but as a *dastgāh*, on the mode of *Śur*, cannot be overlooked.

14 Dastgāh-e Māhur

The intervallic structure of the mode of *Māhur* parallels that of the major mode in western music. Yet, because of the other elements which go into the making of Persian modes, probably no melody in the major mode can be said to be in the mode of *Māhur*. Persian musicians fail to appreciate this fact and are very eager to point out that the major mode is the same as the mode of *Māhur*.[1]

Example 230

Example 230 gives the modal scheme for *Māhur*. The characteristics of this mode are:

1. The range is unusually wide, a minor 10th.
2. The finalis has a central position; it is the linking tone of two conjunct major tetrachords. It is also the usual *āqāz*.
3. The 7th above the finalis is a semi-tone flatter than its lower octave, the 2nd below.
4. Leaps of thirds, both ascending and descending are common.
5. Ascending leaps of perfect fourths are occasionally used. A leap of a perfect fifth from the finalis to the 5th above is rarely used. The use of such leaps makes *Māhur* capable of greater excitement than most other Persian modes. But, the melodic movement is still predominantly step-wise.

Forud

In *dastgāh-e Māhur*, because of its many diverse *gušes*, the role of the *forud* is very significant in binding the whole repertoire together. In the *forud*, the 3rd and the 2nd below receive

Example 231

emphasis, and usually the finalis is approached from below. Example 231 is a typical *forud* of *Māhur*. The finalis may be also approached from above. This type, as shown in example 232,

Example 232

89

is less typical and gives no emphasis to the tetrachord below the finalis. A third type of *forud*, given in example 233, emphasises the four notes above and below the finalis.

Example 233

Darāmads

An authentic style of performance in *dastgāh-e Māhur* customarily begins with an improvisation under the name of *Moqaddame* (introduction) before the *darāmad*s. This *Moqaddame* is sometimes followed by a group of metric pieces, which are of recent origin, and not of sufficient interest or authenticity to be considered here. The *Moqaddame* itself is nearly always included in a performance. It is a stately but unornate declamation which sets the tone for the *dastgāh*, even though its characteristics are not maintained throughout. The *Moqaddame* places more emphasis on the tetrachord below the finalis; its basic melodic pattern is given in example 234. Example 235 (p. 165) is the transcription of an improvisation on this theme.

Example 234

After the *Moqaddame*, the *darāmad* section begins. Here, certain modifications in the mode of *Māhur* are effected. These modifications are:

1. The tetrachord above the finalis receives more emphasis than the tetrachord below it, except in the *forud*.
2. The 2nd above the finalis (d in our scale) becomes the *šāhed*.
3. The 4th above may function as the *āqāz* in place of the finalis.
4. The melodic movement is overwhelmingly diatonic. Rare leaps of thirds are used; larger leaps are avoided, unless between phrases.

The basic formula for a *darāmad* in *Māhur* is given in example 236. An improvisation on this melodic idea is found in example 237 (p. 165).

Example 236

Dastgāh-e Māhur is rich in the number and variety of its *guše*s, many of which modulate to modes very remote from the mode of *Māhur* itself. The major *guše*s are *Dād, Xosrovāni, Tusi,*

Azarbāyejāni, Feyli, Abol, Delkaš, Neyriz, Šekaste, Nahib, Arāq, Āšur, Rāk, Rāk-e Kašmir, and *Rāk-e Hendi.*

Dād

Guše-ye Dād employs the mode of *Māhur* of the *darāmad* area, but with slight modifications, as shown in example 238. The characteristics of this mode are:

1.   The tones below the finalis are omitted.
2.   The concentration is on the 2nd, 3rd and 4th above, and to a lesser degree on the 5th above. The 6th and the 7th above are rarely heard.
3.   The finalis is prominent only at the beginning and in the *forud.*
4.   The 2nd above is the *šāhed* and the *ist.*
5.   The 4th above is the *āqāz.*

Example 238

The basic melodic formula for *Dād* is given in example 239. Example 240 (p. 166) is a transcription of an improvisation on this theme.

Example 239

Xosrovāni

Guše-ye Xosrovāni is in the same mode of *Dād.* Again, the emphasis is on the three tones above the finalis, but the 2nd above is not favoured more than the other two tones and, therefore, is no longer to be considered as the *šāhed.* Its starting note is the 5th above, which is more prominent here than in *Dād.* This *guše* is also performed in *dastgāh-e Bayāt-e Tork.* Since *Xosrovāni* only uses the hexachord above the finalis, and this hexachord is the same in the modes of *Māhur* and *Bayāt-e Tork,* the performance of this *guše* in the two *dastgāhs* can be identical. Only the *forud* will be different.

The basic melodic formula for *Xosrovāni* is as shown in example 241. Example 242 (p. 167) shows an improvisation on this theme.

Example 241

Tusi

In its modal structure, *Tusi* is quite similar to *Xosrovāni*. There is no new characteristic, except that the 6th above is heard more often than before. We see, then, that a gradual push towards the higher register of sound is taking place. As noticed in the case of the other *dastgāh*s this gradual approach to the area of the *ōj* is typical of the order of pieces within the structure of a *dastgāh*.

Example 243 shows the basic melodic formula for *Tusi*, and example 244 (p. 168) shows an improvisation on this melodic idea.

Example 243

Azarbāyejāni

Guše-ye Azarbāyejāni employs the tetrachord above the finalis of *Māhur* with more or less equal emphasis on all tones. It would therefore seem reasonable that it should always be performed right after the *darāmad*s. Although this is entirely possible, it is more often performed after *Tusi*. One cannot find a good reason for this placement, particularly since this means that the gradual climb to the *ōj* is rather negated. Yet this lack of conformity to the expected is a further evidence that in Persian music nothing can be taken as a hard and fast rule, and no rule is without its exception.[2]

The basic melodic formula for *Azarbāyejāni* is given in example 245. An improvisation on this idea is shown in example 246 (p. 169).

Example 245

Feyli

In *guše-ye Feyli* the 5th above the finalis becomes the *šāhed*; the 4th above is also emphasised. A leap of a minor third, from the 3rd to the 5th above, is characteristic of the *Feyli* melody. Example 247 gives the basic skeletal idea of this melody.

Example 247

A marked similarity between the opening motifs of *Azarbāyejāni* and *Feyli* is noticed. They both employ the same rhythmic pattern (♪ ♫♫) and the same ascending notes (c, d, e, f). In *Azarbāyejāni*, however, the ascending line is turned back and the emphasis is placed on the 3rd and the 4th above. In *Feyli*, the ascending line reaches up to the 5th above (g) where it concentrates.

The transcription of an improvisation on this theme appears in example 248 (p. 169).

Abol

In *guše-ye Abol* the centre of melodic activity is shifted to the area of the 4th to the 7th above the finalis of *Māhur*. Since this tetrachord (4th to 7th of *Māhur*) is also a major tetrachord, the tendency is to make the 4th into a new finalis. Consequently, what is achieved is a 'key' modulation to the 4th above of the *Māhur* finalis. The new finalis functions also as the *šāhed* and the *āqāz*. The modal scheme for *Abol* is shown in example 249.

Example 249

Abol, in itself, is a short and melodically undistinguished *guše*, but it is usually accompanied by one or more *tekke*s (e.g. *Zangule* or *Naqme* (see chapter 16)). The result is a group of pieces in the new key which confirm the modulation to the 'key' of the 4th above. At the end of the last piece in the group, the melodic line is taken below the finalis, a *Māhur forud* is added, and thus a return modulation to the original key is accomplished.

Example 250 shows the basic melodic formula for *Abol*, and example 251 (p. 170) is the transcription of an improvisation.

Example 250

Delkaš

One of the most important and striking *guše*s in *dastgāh-e Māhur* is *Delkaš*. It represents an abrupt change of mode from that of *Māhur* to the mode of *Delkaš*, which is an interesting blend of *Šur* and *Māhur*. In *Delkaš*, the pentachord above the finalis of *Māhur* is kept intact, but the 6th above is lowered by a microtone ($a^{\natural}$ to a^{p}). Consequently, the tetrachord from the 5th to the 8th above becomes identical with the tetrachord of *Šur* (g, a^{p}, $b^{\flat}$, c). Since the 5th above (g) becomes the new finalis, the atmosphere of *Šur* is unmistakably established. Yet, the melodic activity is not confined to the tetrachord above this new finalis, and frequently the melodic line moves down within the range of the pentachord of *Māhur*. Consequently, a new modal character exclusive to *Delkaš* is created. The modal scheme for *Delkaš* is shown in example 252.

Example 252

The characteristics of the mode of *Delkaš* are:

1.   It employs a relatively wide range of an octave.
2.   From the 2nd below the finalis to the 4th above, this mode is identical with the mode of *Šur*. From the finalis to the 5th below it is the same as the mode of *Māhur*.
3.   Except for occasional leaps of thirds, its movement is step-wise.
4.   The finalis has a central position in relation to the melodic movement.
5.   The finalis is also the *āqāz*.

Delkaš is usually followed by a *Čahārmezrāb* (see chapter 17) and possibly one or more *tekke*s (see chapter 16). Thus it becomes an important and lengthy section within *dastgāh-e Māhur*.

The basic melodic formula for *Delkaš* is given in example 253, and the transcription of an improvisation on this melodic idea appears in example 254 (p. 170).

Example 253

Neyriz

This *guše* has been discussed in chapter 13, in connection with *dastgāh-e Navā*. The mode of *Neyriz* in *Māhur* is different from that of *Neyriz* in *Navā* in its 3rd degree below the finalis. By referring to the scale of this mode in the previous chapter (example 219), we can see that the interval from the 3rd to the 2nd below is a neutral second (b^p to c). In the mode of *Neyriz* of *Māhur* this interval is a minor second (b^k to c). Example 255 shows the modal scheme for *Neyriz* in *dastgāh-e Māhur*.

Example 255

By using b^k instead of b^p, something of the nature of the mode of *Māhur* itself is retained. In the *forud*, simply by raising the 2nd above e^p to e^k, we are entirely back in the mode of *Māhur*. With the exception just mentioned, the characteristics of this mode are those given in chapter 13; and the basic melodic formula upon which improvisation is made is the same.

It is interesting to note that the finalis of *Delkaš* is the 5th above the finalis of *Māhur*, but in *Neyriz*, which is a similar mode, the 2nd above the finalis of *Māhur* becomes the finalis. It can be speculated that *Delkaš*, being an expressive *guše* with a relatively wide range and much melodic movement, requires a relatively high register of sound. *Neyriz*, on the other hand, is a relatively placid and static *guše* for which a lower register of sound is more suitable.

Šekaste

With *guše-ye Šekaste*, modulation is made to yet another distant mode. The mode of *Šekaste* has strong similarities to that of *Afšāri*.[3] Yet, this seemingly distant modulation is achieved by the simple lowering of the 3rd above the finalis of *Māhur* by a microtone (e to e^p). This alteration was already made in *Neyriz*. Accordingly, the modal scheme for *Šekaste* is as shown in example 256.

Example 256

The characteristics of this mode are those of the mode of *Afšāri* (see chapter 8). The only exception is that the 6th in *Afšāri* is a neutral 6th above the finalis, but as a *moteqayyer*, it is occasionally raised by a microtone (a^p to a^1). The reason for this reversal of the function of the *moteqayyer* in the two modes is that in *Afšāri*, the 6th above is more often used as a neighbouring tone to the 5th, and usually is resolved on to the 5th; therefore, a smaller interval between the two degrees enhances the feeling of the 6th above being drawn to the 5th. In *Šekaste*, on the contrary, more often the 6th above leads to the 7th or 8th, and in this upward pull, a smaller interval between the 6th and 7th degrees becomes more effective.

Melodically, *Šekaste* contains more leaps than may be found in most other *gušes* of *dastgāh-e Māhur*. These leaps, both down and up, originate primarily from the *šāhed* (5th above). They occur downward to the finalis (a perfect 5th), to the 2nd above (a perfect 4th), and to the 3rd above (a neutral 3rd); a leap of a perfect 4th upward to the 8th above is also common. A chromatic half-step trill on the 4th above (f to g^b) is characteristic of *Šekaste*, as has also been seen in *Afšāri*. Whenever this trill is used, the melodic line is in a descending movement, so that the 4th above, after the trill, resolves down to the 3rd above, and never up to the 5th.

The basic melodic formula for *Šekaste* is given in example 257, and a transcription of an improvisation on this idea appears in example 258 (p. 171).

Example 257

Nahib

This *guše* has already been considered as part of the repertoires of *dastgāh-e Afšāri* and *dastgāh-e Navā*. Its discussion, however, has been postponed until now because traditionally it is more readily identified with *dastgāh-e Māhur* than with the other two. While a performance of *Afšāri* or *Navā* may or may not include *Nahib*, in *Māhur* it is invariably performed. The same is true of two other *gušes* which follow *Nahib*, and are modally and melodically related to it: *Arāq* and *Āšur*. These three *gušes* are in the area of the *ōj* of *Māhur*, and constitute the climactic portion of the *dastgāh*. They present a distinct mode of their own, but make use of the *Māhur forud* pattern.[4]

Example 259

The modal scheme for this group of *gušes* appears in example 259. The characteristics of this mode are:

1. The finalis is the same as that of *Māhur*, but it is used only at the beginning and in the *forud*. In the main part of melodic improvisations in these *gušes*, it is not heard at all.
2. The 2nd, 3rd and 4th above the finalis are used only in passing, at the beginning or in the *forud*.
3. The 5th above is the *ist*. All of the musical phrases end on that note, yet it can never satisfy as the finalis.
4. The 7th above is a *moteqayyer*. In ascending movement, and sometimes in descending, it maintains its basic form, which is a major 7th above the finalis. Often, in descending movement, it is lowered by a semi-tone (bᵇ instead of bᵏ).
5. The 8th above is the *šāhed*.
6. The 10th above, as compared with its lower octave (the 3rd above) is a semi-tone flat (eᵇ instead of dᵏ).
7. The area of melodic activity is between the 5th and the 9th above. This pentachord, according to whether the neutral or the flat version of the *moteqayyer* (bᵏ or bᵇ) is used, changes from a major to a minor pentachord.
8. The melodic movement in this mode is overwhelmingly diatonic. Leaps, as a rule, occur only between phrases.

The basic melodic formula for *Nahib* is given in example 260. Example 261 (p. 172) shows the transcription of an improvisation on this melodic idea, concluding with a *Māhur forud*.

Example 260

Arāq

Guše-ye Arāq is but a variation of *Nahib*. In fact, in contemporary practice, the two are often confused with one another. The only significant difference between the two is that in *Arāq*, in the course of an improvisation, the melodic line, by means of sequential patterns, is taken up to the 11th above the finalis. *Arāq*, therefore, is slightly more intense in its emotional content, as it reaches a higher register of sound.

Example 262 (p. 173) shows an improvisation in *Arāq*, which is based on the same melodic formula as shown for *Nahib* (example 260).

Āšur

Āšur is an extension of *Arāq* into an even higher register of sound; here, the melodic line reaches the 12th above the finalis of *Māhur*. In fact, the melodic movement is confined to the area of the 8th to the 12th above. On that basis, we can consider *Āšur* to have its own modal scheme which would be as shown in example 263. In this mode the 8th above the finalis of *Māhur* is the *ist*, and the 11th above is both the *āqāz* and the *šāhed*.

Example 263

We must emphasise, however, that *Āšur* is more in the nature of a high passage in the modal scheme of *Arāq*. The shift of emphasis to the area of the 8th to the 15th above is brief. Soon after *Āšur*, the emphasis is lowered to the area of the 5th to the 9th above, which constitutes a return to the mode of *Nahib-Arāq*.

The basic melodic formula for *Āšur* is given in example 264. Example 265 (p. 174) shows an

Example 264

improvisation in *Āšur*, at the conclusion of which a descent is made into the area of *Nahib-Arāq*.

Rāk

The name of this *guše* is one of the many obscure titles in the *radif* of Persian music. The word is without any meaning in the modern Persian language, but it is probably a Persian pronunciation for the Indian word *Raga*. Why and how this word has come to be used as a title for this *guše* no one knows. The two ensuing *gušes*, *Rāk-e Kašmir* (Kashmiri *Raga*) and *Rāk-e Hendi* (Indian *Raga*) are equally unintelligible. Whether the mode or the themes for these *gušes* are of Indian origin is highly doubtful. The concept of *raga*, as such, is unknown in Persia. Aside from the fact that both Indian and Persian musics are modal, there is no discernible relationship between them. Certainly there is no more connection between these *gušes* with the Indian *Raga* system than between any piece of the Persian *radif* and that system.

The mode of *Rāk*, in its range and the roles of its tones, is very similar to the mode of *Nahib-Arāq*. There are, however, two significant differences between them.

1.   The 6th above, in the mode of *Rāk*, is a neutral sixth to the finalis, and not a major sixth.
2.   The 7th above is not a *moteqayyer*, and remains a major 7th, in relation to the finalis, throughout.

The modal scheme for *Rāk* is shown in example 266a. The characteristics of this mode, as

Example 266a

well as the melodic patterns for *guše-ye Rāk*, are very similar to those of *Nahib*. Therefore, the two differences mentioned above are, in substance, the main points of variance between them. Nevertheless, these two changes unmistakably distinguish *Rāk* from *Nahib*.

It is also noteworthy that the area of melodic concentration in *Rāk*, which is the pentachord from the 5th to the 9th above with emphasis on the 8th, resembles the intervallic structure of the mode of *Čahārgāh* in *dastgāh-e Homāyun* (see chapter 11). This similarity and association with *Čahārgāh* is not found in *Nahib*.

The basic melodic formula for *Rāk* is given in example 266b, and an improvisation on this idea is shown in example 267 (p. 174).

Example 266b

Rāk-e Kašmir

Rāk-e Kašmir is based on the same mode as that of *Rāk*. However, the 8th above the finalis, which is the *šāhed*, is also the *āqāz*. The melodic formula for *Rāk-e Kašmir* is distinct from that of *Rāk*, but it too concentrates on the higher register of the scale. Example 268 shows its basic formula, and example 269 (p. 175) is the transcription of an improvisation on it.

Example 268

Rāk-e Hendi

This *guše* is normally the last piece in the traditional repertoire of *dastgāh-e Māhur*. Its mode bridges the mode of the two preceding *gušes* (*Rāk* and *Rāk-e Kašmir*) with that of *Māhur* itself. In its use of the *ōj* register and emphasis on the 8th above, it is a continuation of the mode of *Rāk*, but the 10th above, here, is now raised (e and not e⁵) and corresponds with the 3rd above in the mode of *Māhur*. Another characteristic of *Rāk-e Hendi* is that it is a metric piece in the linear hemiola rhythm (6/4 + 3/2), so common to rhythmic pieces in Persian music. It is, therefore, more in the nature of a composed piece, or a *zarbi*. Its melodic form is relatively fixed, and is not subject to much change from one performance to another.

Example 270

The modal scheme for *Rāk-e Hendi* is as shown in example 270. The characteristics of this mode are:

1. This mode employs the unusually wide range of a 12th.
2. The 5th above is the *āqāz*.
3. The 8th above is the *ist*, but it is not the *šāhed* as it was in *Rāk*. The 8th and the 9th are both emphasised.
4. The main section of *guše-ye Rāk-e Hendi* employs the area of the 5th to the 12th above. The lowest tetrachord is heard in the concluding phrase, which is much in the order of a *Māhur forud*, but also in the established hemiola rhythm.
5. The 6th above, in the final phrase, is raised by a microtone (aᵖ to aᵏ), so that a decisive conclusion in the mode of *Māhur* is made.

Since this *guše* is not subject to extensive improvisation, a basic melodic formula cannot be extracted. Therefore, a complete notation of its melody has been given in example 271 (p. 175).

Thus, after numerous excursions into other modes but with constant reference to the original mode of the *dastgāh*, we are now back in *Māhur*. The conclusion of the performance may include a *Masnavi* (see chapter 16), a *čahārmezrāb*, or a *reng* (see chapter 17).

15   *Dastgāh-e Rāst (Rāst-Panjgāh)*

The least performed of the twelve *dastgāh*s is *Rāst-Panjgāh*. This neglect is due to the fact that the greater portion of the *radif* of this *dastgāh* is taken from the repertoire of other *dastgāh*s. Some Persian musicians are of the opinion that this *dastgāh* has evolved for pedagogic purposes, in the study of which the skill of modulation to many diverse modes is cultivated.[1]

In our present discussion, the word *Panjgāh* is omitted from the title of this *dastgāh*. This is not done for convenience alone. The curious fact is that one of the *guše*s of this *dastgāh* is named *Panjgāh*, and that this *guše* is not in the mode of *Rāst*, but is the mode of *Šur*. It would seem unreasonable, therefore, to be discussing the mode of *Rāst-Panjgāh*, when *Panjgāh* as a *guše* in the *dastgāh*, has a different mode. The name of this *dastgāh* is one more example of the irregularities one encounters in the *dastgāh* system.

It is of some significance that *Rāst* is the title of a mode (*maqām*) mentioned in all medieval treatises. Also, in the related musical traditions of Turkey and the Arabic-speaking countries, one invariably finds a mode by the name *Rāst*. But the medieval sources do not give us a *Panjgāh* mode and rarely does the name appear in musical systems outside today's Persia.

In its intervallic structure, the mode of *Rāst* is identical with that of *Māhur*. In this respect also, this *dastgāh* lacks independence of identity. Therefore, since in its repertoire, and in the structure of its intervals, *Rāst* is dependent on other *dastgāh*s, it is not difficult to see why it is not a favoured *dastgāh*.

Although the mode of *Rāst* employs the same intervals as the mode of *Māhur*, it is always performed in a 'key' a perfect 5th below that of *Māhur*. On most traditional instruments and in vocal practice, *Māhur* is ordinarily performed with c as the finalis. *Rāst* is ordinarily performed with f as the finalis. The relative depth of the sound register contributes to the quality of dignity which is attributed to this mode.

Example 272

The modal scheme for *Rāst* is given in example 272. The characteristics of this mode are:

1.   The finalis is also the *āqāz*.
2.   Most of the melodic activity takes place above the finalis. The 2nd above is particularly prominent.
3.   The tetrachord below the finalis is less emphasised than in the mode of *Māhur*. It is particularly significant that the 4th below has a non-essential role, whereas in *Māhur*, this degree is very prominent. This contributes measurably to the distinctiveness of improvisations in *Māhur* and in *Rāst*.
4.   The melodic movement is overwhelmingly step-wise.

100

Forud

Since in its repertoire, and in its mode, *Rāst* is largely dependent upon other *dastgāh*s, its identity as a *dastgāh* hinges almost solely on its *forud* patterns. In the course of a performance of *dastgāh-e Rāst*, in some areas, it would be difficult to know which *dastgāh* is being performed, were it not for the use of its very distinctive *forud* patterns. These *forud* patterns are often lengthy and elaborate. A typical *Rāst forud* is almost a piece in its own right and may take as long as a minute to perform.

The *Rāst forud* usually starts on the 4th above, moves within the area of the finalis to the 6th above, and often concludes with the *Bāl-e Kabutar* motif. In *Rāst*, this motif involves a leap of a perfect 5th up, from the finalis to the 5th, and down to the finalis (see example 273). Before

Example 273

the *Bāl-e Kabutar*, the finalis is approached from the 2nd below, or the 3rd and the 2nd below. Example 274 is an example of a *Rāst forud*. An abbreviated version of this *forud*, using the

Example 274

material from the final portion of the above pattern is occasionally used, as shown by example 275.

Example 275

Darāmads

The melodic basis for the *darāmad*s of *Rāst* rests on two phrases. In the first phrase, the finalis has a central position. The improvisation moves first within the tetrachord below, and next in the pentachord above the finalis. The use of a motivic sequence is the main tool for melodic expansion. Example 276 gives the basic formula for part one of the *darāmad* theme. In the 2nd phrase of the *darāmad*, the tetrachord below the finalis loses its significance and the impro-

Example 276

visation concentrates on the pentachord above, with special emphasis on the 2nd above (see example 277).

Example 277

Of the two phrases, the second one has more scope and diversity, and is more representative of the mode of *Rāst*. We can see that even though the intervallic structure in the modes of *Māhur* and *Rāst* are the same, their melodic forms are not. An improvisation on the *darāmad* theme given here will never be confused with a *darāmad* of *Māhur*.

A transcription of an improvisation utilising both phrases of the *darāmad* theme of *Rāst* is given in example 278 (p. 175).

It has already been noted that the majority of *gušes* performed in *dastgāh-e Rāst* are taken from other *dastgāh*s, which explains why this *dastgāh* is the last one in our present study. These *gušes*, as well as the few which are the exclusive property of *dastgāh-e Rāst* itself, are listed here in the order in which they are most commonly performed: *Parvāne, Xosrovāni, Ruhafzā, Neyriz, Zābol, Panjgāh, Qarače, Mobarqa', Sepehr, Nahib, Arāq, Āšur, Abolčap, Tarz, Leyli-o Mejnun, Nōruzhā, Nafir, Māvarāonnahr, Rāk, Rāk-e Kašmir* and *Rāk-e Hendi*.

Of these *gušes, Parvāne, Ruhafzā, Sepehr, Panjgāh, Mobarqa'* and *Māvarāonnahr* belong to *dastgāh-e Rāst. Xosrovāni, Rāk, Rāk-e Kašmir* and *Rāk-e Hendi* are taken from *dastgāh-e Māhur; Abolčap, Tarz, Leyli-o Majnun, Nōruzhā* and *Nahir* come from the repertoire of *Dastgāh-e Homāyun; Zābol* is taken from *dastgāh-e Segāh*, and *Qarače* comes from *dastgāh-e Šur. Neyriz, Nahib, Arāq* and *Ašur* are more vagrant and, as we have seen, they can be performed in any number of *dastgāh*s.

Parvāne

Parvāne is a very brief *guše* with a short melodic phrase which is often performed without many improvised additions. The *āqāz* for *Parvāne* is the 3rd above. Its melodic line moves step-wise to the 7th above, then descends to the finalis. The 5th above is the most emphasised tone. The basic melodic formula for *Parvāne* is given in example 279. An improvisation on this theme is shown in example 280 (p. 176).

Example 279

Xosrovāni

This *guše* has been discussed in chapter 14 on *dastgāh-e Māhur*. It is used here quite in the same way as in *Māhur*, except that it is in the 'key' of f instead of c. For musical examples of *Xosrovāni*, see chapter 14.

Ruhafzā

Guše-ye Ruhafzā presents two musical phrases as its thematic material. The first of these is clearly in the mode of *Rāst* with the 5th above as the *āqāz*. In the second phrase the 3rd above the finalis is lowered by a microtone (a♮ to a♭). As a result of this change, through the tetrachord (g-a♭-b♭-c), the mode of *Šur* is momentarily suggested, helping to pave the way for the appearance of *guše-ye Neyriz*, which is to follow.

Example 281

Considering both phrases of *Ruhafzā*, its modal scheme is as shown in example 281. The characteristics of this mode are:

1. The finalis is the lowest note.
2. The 3rd above the finalis is a *moteqayyer*.
3. The 5th above is the *āqāz*.
4. The 7th above is raised by a half-step (e♭ to e♮) only in one place, in the second phrase of *Ruhafzā*, when the line moves up rapidly to the 8th above. Because of this upward resolution, the use of e♮ and the resultant semi-tone e to f, seems more satisfying.
5. The melodic movement is basically step-wise, but leaps of thirds are occasionally used.

The basic melodic formulae for the two phrases of *Ruhafzā* are shown in example 282. A transcription of an improvisation in *Ruhafzā* is shown in example 283 (p. 176).

Example 282

Neyriz

Guše-ye Neyriz was discussed in chapter 13 in connection with *dastgāh-e Navā*. Its mode is affiliated with that of *Šur*, and in *dastgāh-e Rāst*, the 2nd above the finalis of *Rāst* becomes the new finalis. The 2nd above this finalis is lowered by a microtone (this change of aᵏ to aᴾ had been briefly effected in the second phrase of *Ruhafzā*, see example 282) and functions as the *šāhed*. The 3rd below the new finalis is lowered by a microtone also (eᵏ to eᴾ), to correspond with the 3rd below in the mode of *Šur*, and acts as the *āqāz*. Thus, the mode of *Neyriz* in *dastgāh-e Rāst* takes on the scheme given in example 284. For musical examples of *guše-ye Neyriz*, see chapter 13.

Example 284

Zābol

From the mode of *Neyriz*, particularly since the 2nd above in *Neyriz* is the *šāhed*, modulation to *Zābol* is easily accomplished. The mode of *Zābol* has been discussed in chapter 9. The only difference between the *Zābol* here and that described in *dastgāh-e Segāh*, is that here it is based on aᴾ as the finalis instead of eᴾ, which was the finalis for the mode *Segāh*. The modal scheme for *Zābol* in *dastgāh-e Rāst* is, therefore, as shown in example 285. We note that the

Example 285

modulation from *Neyriz* to *Zābol* is fundamentally a matter of change of emphasis and a climb to a higher note within the same scale.

For musical examples of *Zābol*, refer to chapter 9.

Panjgāh

It is ironic that *guše-ye Panjgāh*, which has contributed its name to the title of the *dastgāh* presently under discussion, is merely a short piece, and is decisively in the mode of *Šur*. Why this *guše*, with no distinctive identity of mode or melody, has a name which follows the title of two of the twelve *dastgāh*s (*Segāh* and *Čahārgāh*), is equally baffling. (More has been said about the use of the word '*gāh*' as a musical term in connection with *guše-ye Dogāh*, in chapter 7).

The mode established with *Neyriz* and briefly interrupted by *Zābol* is re-established for *Panjgāh*. Certain modifications, however, are made. The 3rd below the finalis no longer functions as the *āqāz*; instead, the 2nd below is the *āqāz*. There is no *šāhed*, and the melodic movement is mostly confined to the tetrachord above the finalis. All of these characteristics correspond with those of the mode of *Šur*. Example 286 gives the modal scheme for *Panjgāh*.

Example 286

The basic melodic formula for *Panjgāh* is shown in example 287, and an improvisation on this idea is shown in example 288 (p. 177).

Example 287

Qarače

As in *dastgāh-e Šur*, from which this *guše* is taken, *Qarače* is in the mode of *Šur* but in the 'key' of the 4th above the finalis. Our musical examples of *Šur* (chapter 4) were based on the tone d as the finalis; and *Qarače* was consequently based on the tone g as its finalis. In *Dastgāh-e Rāst*, the *gušes* which were in the mode of *Šur* have been based on the tone g as their finalis; *Qarače* is based on the same mode but on the 4th above (c) as its finalis. Thus the modal scheme for *Qarače* will be as shown in example 289. For musical examples of *Qarače*, refer to chapter 4.

Example 289

Mobarqa'

Mobarqa' is a short *guše* which functions as a transitional piece for modulation from the mode of *Qarače* back to that of *Rāst*. It begins with the 2nd above the finalis of *Qarače* as its *āqāz*. Shortly after that, it moves to the 4th above (f), which is the 8th above the finalis of *Rāst*, and immediately thereafter, the mode of *Rāst* is re-established by cancelling out the alterations which the mode of *Qarače* had imposed (d^p to d^i, e^b to e^s). The use of e^s instead of e^b, which is the normal 7th above in *Rāst*, is due to that note's inclination to resolve to the 8th above, and the fact that a semi-tone relationship between them provides a more satisfying resolution.

Mobarqa' concentrates in the area of the 5th to the 8th above the finalis of *Rāst*. The 8th above is the *šāhed* and the *ist*. Example 290 gives the modal scheme of *Mobarqa'*. The basic

Example 290

melodic formula for *Mobarqa'* is shown in example 291, and a transcription of an improvisation on this theme is given in example 292 (p. 177).

Example 291

Sepehr

Guše-ye Sepehr is in the mode of *Rāst*; however, the centre of melodic activity, as in *Mobarqa'*, is in the area of the 5th up to the 10th above the finalis of *Rāst*. At the conclusion of *Sepehr*, a descent to the tetrachord above the finalis, and the addition of a *Rāst forud*, firmly re-establishes the original mode of *Rāst*.

The basic melodic formula for *Sepehr* is shown in example 293. A transcription of an improvisation in *Sepehr* is shown in example 294 (p. 178).

Example 293

Nahib, *Arāq* and *Āšur*

These three *gušes*, which are related modally and melodically to one another, have been discussed in chapter 14, in connection with *dastgāh-e Māhur*. In *dastgāh-e Rāst* they are performed with f as their finalis instead of c, which was the finalis in *dastgāh-e Māhur*. In every other respect, they are virtually the same pieces.

The mode of *Nahib* in *dastgāh-e Rāst* has the scheme given in example 295.

Example 295

After *Āšur*, a second improvisation in *guše-ye Parvāne*, with an extended *Rāst forud*, is usually performed. This practice helps to recall the original mode of *Rāst*, which had been neglected, and will be set aside once again with the following *gušes*.

Abolčap, *Tarz* and *Leyli-o Majnun*

These three *gušes* come from the *radif* of *dastgāh-e Homāyun*. For their description and for musical examples, refer to chapter 11. In *dastgāh-e Homāyun*, according to our notation, they were based on the tone g as their finalis, and c as the *šāhed*. In *dastgāh-e Rāst*, f, which has been the finalis, becomes the *šāhed*, and c is the finalis. Accordingly, in order to recreate the mode of *Abolčap*, *Tarz* and *Leyli-o Majnun*, a is lowered to a♭ and d is lowered to dᵖ. These alterations are made without a modulation; that is to say, after *Parvāne*, *Abolčap* is presented quite abruptly. Example 296 shows the modal scheme for *Abolčap* in *dastgāh-e Rāst*.

Example 296

Nōruzhā and *Nafir*

Nōruz-e Arab, *Nōruz-e Sabā*, *Nōruz-e Xārā*, and *Nafir* are related pieces which are part of the *radif* of *dastgāh-e Homāyun*. In *Homāyun*, the 4th above the finalis becomes the new finalis for these *gušes*. In *dastgāh-e Rāst*, the 8th above (the *šāhed* in *Abolčap*, *Tarz* and *Leyli-o Majnun*) becomes the finalis. Since most of the melodic activity in *Nōruzhā* and in *Nafir* centres above the finalis, these *gušes* will constitute the *ōj* of *dastgāh-e Rāst*. Example 297 gives the modal

Example 297

scheme for *Nōruzhā* in *dastgāh-e Rāst*. For musical examples of the *Nōruzhā* and *Nafir*, see chapter 11.

Māvarāonnahr

Māvarāonnahr is the last *guše* in *dastgāh-e Rāst* which belongs to its own *radif*, and is not taken from another *dastgāh*. But, alas, it is not in the mode of *Rāst* but is another improvisation in the mode of *Nōruzhā*. It does, however, extend the melodic line to as high as e♭ and, as such, becomes the highest-reaching *guše* of the *dastgāh*. The 5th above the finalis is the *āqāz*. All other characteristics of *Māvarāonnahr* are those of *Nōruzhā* and *Nafir*, which have preceded it. We may ask, then, why is it exclusive to *dastgāh-e Rāst*? Unfortunately, no satisfactory answer can be found, other than the fact that this is how the tradition has evolved.

Example 298 shows the basic melodic formula for *Māvarāonnahr*, and an improvisation on this melodic idea is given in example 299 (p. 178).

Example 298

Rākhā

As in the case of *dastgāh-e Māhur*, *Rāk*, *Rāk-e Kašmir* and *Rāk-e Hendi* are the last *gušes* to be performed in *dastgāh-e Rāst*. For descriptions and musical examples of *Rākhā*, the reader is referred to chapter 14. Their modal scheme in *dastgāh-e Rāst* is given in example 300.

Example 300

The individual pieces within each group of related *gušes* do not refer back to the original mode of the *dastgāh* by means of a *forud*. But, after the last *guše* in each group, ordinarily a *forud* of *Rāst* is included. Following the very last piece in the *dastgāh*, which is usually *Rāk-e Hendi*, an extensive *forud* of *Rāst* is commonly performed, so that the conclusion of this *dastgāh* may be in the framework of its basic mode.

Although the use of pieces from the *radif* of other *dastgāh*s is common to almost all of the *dastgāh*s, it is the *radif* of *Rāst* alone which is largely composed of such pieces. It is not, therefore, a very independent *dastgāh*; but it is very colourful and well worth listening to.

16 Vagrant *gušes*

Study of the twelve *dastgāh*s has shown that the *radif* of each *dastgāh* includes pieces that are exclusive to it, and also some that are taken from the *radif* of other *dastgāh*s. There is still another group of pieces that are performed, or can be performed, in all of the *dastgāh*s. The pieces in this group have relatively stable melodic and rhythmic structures and are not subject to extensive change through improvisation. More important is the fact that they have no modal stability. They adopt the mode of the *dastgāh* in which they are placed, or even the mode of *gušes* which have preceded them. As such, while the melodic and the rhythmic identities of these pieces are preserved, their modes change according to where they are placed. The word *tekke* (small or short piece) will be used here to identify this genre of *guše*. Writers on Persian music have generally failed to recognise that, due to their instability and adaptability, these pieces must necessarily be placed in a separate category. At times they are identified simply as *zarbi* or rhythmic pieces.

There are two types of *tekke*: those that have a more or less clear and stable metric structure and are exclusively instrumental (we shall call this group rhythmic *tekke*s); and those that do not have a stable metric basis and can be performed vocally as well as on instruments (we shall call this group non-rhythmic *tekke*s).

Rhythmic *tekke*s

Kerešme

This is the most commonly performed of *tekke*s. In one place or another it is played in every *dastgāh*. The most significant aspect of a *kerešme* is its metric structure which is invariably a linear hemiola: a very regular alternation of duple and triple metres (6/4, 3/2 or 6/8, 3/4), is the rule.

Melodically, *kerešme* centres around the first tetrachord of the mode in which it is placed; it is step-wise in movement, with occasional leaps of fourths and thirds.

In their modes, *kerešme*s yield entirely to the *dastgāh*, or a *guše* of the *dastgāh*, in which they are performed. For comparison, transcriptions of ten different *kerešme*s in different modes are given in examples 301–10:

> Example 301 (p. 179) in the mode of *Šur*
> Example 302 (p. 179) in the mode of *Bayāt-e Tork*
> Example 303 (p. 179) in the mode of *Segāh*
> Example 304 (p. 180) in the mode of *guše-ye Hesār* of *Segāh*
> Example 305 (p. 180) in the mode of *Čahārgāh*
> Example 306 (p. 180) in the mode of *guše-ye Maqlub* of *Čahārgāh*
> Example 307 (p. 181) in the mode of *Homāyun*

Example 308 (p. 181) in the mode of *Bayāt-e Esfahān*
Example 309 (p. 181) in the mode *guše-ye Arāq* of *Rāst*
Example 310 (p. 182) in the mode of *Navā*.

Bastenegār

Bastenegār is a mere passage or exercise which may be played freely as a part of an improvisation, and as such it can be introduced in various places. Although it is not performed in a strict metre, a duple pulse predominates, and the tempo is fast. The melodic pattern begins on the *šāhed* of the mode and, with a consistently step-wise movement, moves up and then returns to the *šāhed*.

Example 311 (p. 182) shows a *bastenegār* in the mode of *Abuatā*.

A *bastenegār* may be introduced abruptly or it may be preceded by a short rhapsodic phrase based on its opening motif (see example 312 (p. 182), in the mode of *guše-ye Zābol* of *Čahārgāh*).

As is the case with many of these short rhythmic *tekke*s, *bastenegār* does not take on the form of a piece by maintaining its melodic and rhythmic character to a clear ending; rather it simply dissolves into a free and rhapsodic section which is a continuation of the *guše* to which *bastenegār* has seemingly been attached (see example 313 (p. 182), in the mode of *Afšāri*.

Naqme

Naqme does not suggest one clear form, and in the practice of Persian music three different types of *tekke*s are called by this name.[1] In the collection of the *radif* by Ma'rufi,[2] fourteen *naqme*s have been given. Four of these are clearly *kerešne*-type pieces, with the characteristic linear hemiola metre. This sort of confusion in Ma'rufi's collection is not uncommon. It is indicative not so much of the disorderliness of the collection, but the fact that a certain type of piece may traditionally be known under two different names. One of the *naqme*s which is notated in *Navā* has absolutely no melodic significance of its own and is decidedly a mere continuation of the *darāmad* section of the *dastgāh*.

One *naqme* given in *Rāst* has a slow 3/4 melody which is unique and is nearly always included in a performance of *Rāst*. It begins on the 3rd above the finalis of *Rāst* and concludes on the finalis. In an ordinary performance, this *tekke* may simply be called a *zarbi* of *Rāst* (see example 314, p. 182).

Two of the *naqme*s in Ma'rufi's collection are related to one another and both are in the mode of *guše-ye Maqlub*, one in *Segāh* and the other in *Čahārgāh*. They are both in 2/4 metre and in a moderately fast tempo. This type of *naqme* is characterised by large leaps from the high melodic line to the low drone strings (see example 315 (p. 183), *Naqme* in *Segāh*).

Six of the *naqme*s in Ma'rufi's collection are related to one another. They are in fairly stable metric patterns of 3/8, 6/16. Ma'rufi's notation suggests a free metre but the transcriptions that I have made establish them in a stable linear hemiola metre. In every case, except in *Šur*, the *āqāz* is the 2nd below the finalis of the mode; in *Šur* it is the 3rd above (see example 316 (p. 183), *Naqme* in *Māhur*).

Zangule

This is a short rhythmic passage in 3/4 or 3/8. It is commonly played in all of the *dastgāh*s. It has a sequential and step-wise movement and is based on two simple motifs which may become subject to minor variations. Two examples of *Zangule* are given (see example 317 (p. 183), in *Māhur*, and example 318 (p. 184), in *Čahārgāh*).

Dotāyeki

This is a short piece in 2/4 and most commonly played in *Māhur*, *Rāst* and *Čahārgāh*. It is in the nature of an exercise with the use of the drone string on the strong beat (see example 319 p. 184), *Dotāyeki* in *Čahārgāh*).

Non-rhythmic *tekke*s

Hazin

Hazin is based on a relatively stable melodic pattern but with no modal independence. A repeated note motif characterises this *tekke*. The main melodic section of *hazin* encompasses the range of a minor 6th. Within this range the *āqāz*, as a rule, is the 4th above the finalis which is often also the *šāhed* of the mode.

Example 320 (p. 184) and example 321 (p. 185) are both from the *dastgāh-e Navā*. The first example shows *hazin* in the mode of *Navā* itself, while the second is in the mode of *Arāq* which is an important *guše* performed in *dastgāh-e Navā* but possessing its own mode (see chapter 13).

Two other examples show the flexibility with which the comparatively stable melodic form of *Hazin* can adjust to diverse modes (see example 322 (p. 185), *Hazin* in *Šur*; and example 323 (p. 186), *Hazin* in *Čahārgāh*).

Dobeyti

As the name of this *tekke* (two-line verse) implies, its origins must be in vocal tradition, although it is also performed as an instrumental piece. It can be placed in almost any *dastgāh* or *guše* of a *dastgāh*, as it adjusts to any modal requirement. Its melodic form is vaguely fixed; a descending step-wise movement, with intricate ornamentation again suggestive of vocal tradition, characterises this *tekke*. (See examples 324 (p. 186), *Dobeyti* in *Abuatā*, and example 325 (p. 186), *Dobeyti* in *Bayāt-e Esfahān*.)

Jāmedarān

This is a relatively brief *tekke* which is commonly played in *Homāyun*, *Bayāt-e Esfahān*, *Afšāri* and *Bayāt-e Tork*, but can also be played in the other *dastgāh*s. Its main melodic identity lies in the opening phrase which involves the interval of the minor 2nd. Thus, in *Homāyun*, the phrase will begin on the 5th above the finalis and moves to the 6th; in *Bayāt-e Esfahān*, it begins on the 2nd and goes to the 3rd above; in *Afšāri* it begins on the raised form of the 6th and goes to the 7th above; and so on. A descending sequential pattern then follows. (See example 326 (p. 187), *Jāmedarān* in *Afšāri*.)

As this *tekke*, in its modal structure, yields to the mode of the *dastgāh* in which it is placed, the same three phrases of the above example have been given in example 327 (p. 187), as they adapt to the mode of *Homāyun*. For further comparisons, the transcription of a lengthy improvisation in *Jāmedarān*, in the mode of *Bayāt-e Esfahān*, has been given in example 328 (p. 187).

Masnavi

As the name of this *tekke* implies, it has come into the Persian musical tradition by way of poetry.[3] As such, it is primarily a vocal piece, although it may be played by instruments as well. It is frequently a lengthy piece and on that basis it is not altogether logical to include it among the *tekke*s. However, since it is the only piece of some length which does not maintain a fixed mode, it has been included in this chapter. All other large pieces (*gušes*) retain their modal identity regardless of the *dastgāh* in which they may be placed. (An exception to this rule is the body of pieces which appear both in *Segāh* and *Čahārgāh*. See chapters 9 and 10.)

Masnavi can be sung in any of the *dastgāh*s, but it is more common to *Afšāri*, *Bayāt-e Tork*, *Šur*, *Homāyun* and *Bayāt-e Esfahān*. More than in any other, *Masnavi* belongs in *dastgāh-e Afšāri*. Here it is called *Masnavi Pič*, or 'twisted' *Masnavi*. It tends to be lengthier than in any other *dastgāh*. Also, when *Masnavi* is being sung by itself without being preceded by all the other *gušes* of a *dastgāh* (and this is frequently done in reciting the poetry of Jalāladdin Rumi), it is sung in the mode of *Afšāri*.

Masnavi Pič is characterised by an upward leap of a 5th at the beginning of the piece. Subsequent to this leap, the melodic pattern is step-wise and downward. Thus the main body of the piece lies among the first five tones of the mode. However, *Masnavi Pič* has a middle section where the melody moves up from the 5th to the 8th above the finalis and beyond. After this section a return is made to the area of the lower pentachord of the mode. See example 329 (p. 188), *Masnavi Pič* in *Afšāri*.

Other *Masnavi*s performed in other *dastgāh*s have a decided melodic connection with *Masnavi Pič*, although the leap of a 5th at the beginning may be modified. In *Šur*, for example, the leap is a 4th from the 2nd below to the 3rd above the finalis. See example 330 (p. 189), beginning of *Masnavi* in *Šur*.

Another example of *Masnavi* is the transcription of one in *Bayāt-e Esfahān*, shown in example 331 (p. 189). Here the polarity is between the 4th below and the finalis. Occasionally the melodic line transcends the area of the finalis to as high as the 4th above. The beginning upward leap, as in *Šur*, is a 4th, with a subsequent descending step-wise movement.

17 Compositional forms

The main body of Persian classical music is the *radif* of traditional pieces, which are subject to extensive variation through improvisation, as has been shown in the preceding chapters. Recent developments, dating back only to the late nineteenth century, have added a new genre of pieces to the classical repertoire. These pieces differ from the traditional body of the *radif* in three ways: they are composed pieces of more or less defined form; they are rhythmically stable, and fall into regular metric patterns; they are mostly composed by known contemporary musicians, and, as such, they represent an ever-expanding repertoire.

These compositions fall into three instrumental categories: *pišdarāmad*, *reng* and *Čahār-mezrāb*; and one vocal form, the *tasnif or tarāne*.

Pišdarāmad

In the late nineteenth century, as a result of influences from Europe, Persian musicians became interested in group playing. Since the overwhelming bulk of traditional music is improvisatory and cannot be effectively rendered by more than one person at a time, a need for compositions with fixed melodic and rhythmic form was keenly felt. As a response to this need, an instrumental form called *pišdarāmad* was introduced. This innovation has been attributed to Qolām Hoseyn Darviš (1872–1926), a famous *tār* player and a gifted composer.

A *pišdarāmad* is intended as an overture to precede the *darāmad* section of the *dastgāh*, and the name simply means pre-*darāmad*, or pre-opening. It is a composed piece in a set metre, with its melodic ideas drawn from the *darāmad*s and some of the *guše*s of the *dastgāh* for which it is composed. A *pišdarāmad*, therefore, uses not only the basic mode of the *dastgāh*, but also the modes and the melodic ideas of some of the main *guše*s in that *dastgāh*. Accordingly, as the *dastgāh* includes modulations to other modes, the *pišdarāmad* for the *dastgāh* also contains those modulations.

Rhythmically, a *pišdarāmad* may be in duple, triple and, less commonly, in quadruple meter. Its tempo is normally moderate, and its performance may run from one to three minutes.

In order to illustrate the relationship of a *pišdarāmad* to the *dastgāh* for which it is composed, an analysis of the structure of a *pišdarāmad*, composed by Nasrollāh Zarrinpanje for *dastgāh-e Homāyun*[1] (refer to Chapter 11), is given here.

This *pišdarāmad* has fifty-four measures of 2/4, and consists of four sections (example 332, p. 190).

Section I Measures 1–19, in the mode of *Homāyun* (*darāmad*s) containing six short phrases:
a.   Four measures (1–4). The phrase begins and ends with the *šāhed* (the 2nd above the finalis), its range is that of a fourth, from the 3rd below to the 2nd above, which

corresponds to the same range in the opening phrase of a *Homāyun darāmad*. The rhythmic pattern is: ♫ ♫♩ ♩ ♫ ‖ .

b.   Four measures (5–8). This phrase has the same range as phrase 'a', and begins on the *šāhed* but ends on the *ist* (2nd below), which is a characteristic ending in *Homāyun*. This phrase contains two smaller units of two measures each, the second one of which is a melodic sequence of the first, at a step lower. The rhythmic pattern is: ♬♬ ♬♬♩ ♩ 𝄽 ‖ .

c.   Three measures (9–11). This phrase begins on the *ist* and ends on the *šāhed*, but takes the range up one note to the 3rd above. The rhythmic pattern is a mix of phrase 'a' and phrase 'b': ♬♬ ♬♬♩ ♫ ♫♩ ♩ 𝄽 ‖ .

d.   Three measures (12–14). This phrase takes the range up to the 5th above and ends on the *šāhed*. By virtue of its range and its central position, phrase 'd' is the climactic portion within section I. Rhythmically, it is identical with phrase 'c'. The last two measures of 'c' and 'd' are also melodically identical.

e.   Three measures (15–17). This phrase also ends on the *šāhed*, but contracts the range to that of a fourth (2nd below to 3rd above). The rhythmic pattern is: ♬♬♩ ♫♩ ♫♬♩ ♩ 𝄽 ‖ .

f.   Two measures (18 and 19). This short phrase constitutes a brief *forud* on the *ist*. The rhythmic pattern is: ♬♬♩ ♫ ♩ 𝄽 ‖ .

Section II   Measures 20–35, in the mode of *Čakāvak*, contain three phrases:

a.   Five measures (20–4). In *Čakāvak*, the 4th above the finalis of *Homāyun* becomes the *šāhed*, as well as the *āqāz* and the *ist*. Consequently, this phrase begins and ends on that note and places considerable emphasis on it. Its range is from the finalis to the 5th above. The rhythm is based on: ♬♬♩ ♫♩ ♫♫ ♫♫ pattern.

b.   Six measures (25–30). This begins on the 5th, goes as high as the 6th and ends on the 2nd above. Rhythmically, it resembles phrase 'e' of section I. This phrase is composed of two 3-measure phrases, the second of which is a melodic sequence of the first, at a step lower.

c.   Five measures (31–5). This phrase constitutes a return of emphasis on the finalis of *Homāyun*, and can be considered as a *forud* in *Homāyun*. Rhythmically, it is founded on the previously established patterns of sixteenth and eighth notes.

Section III   Measures 36–43, in the mode of *Bidād*, containing two phrases:

a.   Four measures (36–9). In *Bidād*, the 5th above the finalis is the *šāhed*, and in this phrase that note is the ending as well as the most emphasised tone. The range is from the 3rd to the 7th above. Both the finalis and the *šāhed* of *Homāyun*, which are of lesser significance in *Bidād*, have been omitted. Rhythmically, sixteenth and eighth notes prevail.

b.   Four measures (40–3). The last two measures of this phrase are the same as the last two of phrases 'a'. In the first measure, however, the range is extended to the 8th above.

Section IV   Measures 44–54, a return to the mode of *Homāyun*, containing two phrases:

a.   Six measures (44–9). This phrase contains three 2-measure phrases which are sequential in descending movement. It begins on the 5th above and ends on the *šāhed* of *Homāyun*. The mode of *Homāyun* is thus re-established. The range is from the finalis to the 7th above. The rhythmic pattern is: 𝅘𝅥𝅯𝅘𝅥𝅯𝅘𝅥 𝅘𝅥𝅯𝅘𝅥𝅯𝅘𝅥|𝅘𝅥𝅯 𝅘𝅥𝅯 ‖ .

b.   Five measures (50–4). This is the *forud* phrase with a function similar to that of phrase 'c' of section II. With its use, not only a modal unity but a melodic unity is provided for the whole piece.

The use of a *pišdarāmad* is optional. A solo performance of a *dastgāh* seldom begins with a *pišdarāmad*. A group performance, on the other hand, very frequently makes use of this form. It is thus played by the whole ensemble in unison and octaves, with the *tombak* (classical drum) elaborating on the rhythm and keeping it firmly established. After the *pišdarāmad*, the individual instrumentalists improvise separately, and finally conclude the *dastgāh* with a *reng*, which again allows the group to play together. In vocal performances, if an ensemble is used for accompaniment, again a *pišdarāmad* may begin the *dastgāh*. The singer enters after the *pišdarāmad* and is accompanied by individual instruments from the ensemble. A vocal performance usually ends, not with a *reng*, but with a *tasnif*.

Reng

Reng has a much older tradition than the *pišdarāmad*. The word *reng* signifies a dance in the classical style. There is a limited number of *reng*s which come into the repertoire of each *dastgāh* possibly from the nineteenth century or earlier. This group has no known composers.[2] From early in the twentieth century to the present, the repertoire of *reng* has grown, and all of these recent additions have been made by known composers. All of the old *reng*s, and by far most of the new ones, are in a fast 6/8 rhythm.

The compound duple metre, as in 6/8, is extremely prevalent in Persian music. This is true of metric pieces within the classical *radif*, as well as a great majority of folk songs and dances. Besides the straight 6/8 metre, the linear hemiola pattern of 6/8 + 3/4 is also very common, both in folk and in classical music. A basic rhythmic pattern, which in effect embodies both 6/8 and 3/4 metre, is called *šir-e mādar* (mother's milk), and has the following elemental formula: 𝅘𝅥𝅯𝅘𝅥𝅯𝅘𝅥 𝅘𝅥𝅯 𝅘𝅥 ‖ .

The second half of this formula may be varied so that the pattern may appear as: 𝅘𝅥𝅯𝅘𝅥𝅯𝅘𝅥 𝄽 𝅘𝅥., 𝅘𝅥𝅯𝅘𝅥𝅯𝅘𝅥 𝅘𝅥𝅯𝅘𝅥𝅯𝅘𝅥, 𝅘𝅥𝅯𝅘𝅥𝅯𝅘𝅥 𝅘𝅥𝅯𝅘𝅥𝅯𝅘𝅥, 𝅘𝅥𝅯𝅘𝅥𝅯𝅘𝅥 𝅘𝅥𝅯𝅘𝅥𝅯𝅘𝅥𝅘𝅥𝅯𝅘𝅥𝅯, 𝅘𝅥𝅘𝅥𝅯𝅘𝅥𝅯𝅘𝅥, etc. In these patterns, while essentially a pulsation of 6 is maintained, the accent comes on beats 1 and 5, instead of 1 and 4 which is the norm for a compound duple metre. As such, this formula can easily accommodate a piece which is in 6/8 but often includes some measures in 3/4.

All of the *reng*s which are in 6/8 employ the *šir-e mādar* formula as their basic rhythmic pattern.

The form of *reng* resembles that of *pišdarāmad*. In its beginning section, a *reng* also employs melodic ideas related to, or suggestive of, the *darāmad*s of the *dastgāh* for which it is composed. In the middle section, melodic ideas suggestive of one or more of the important *guše*s of the *dastgāh* are used. And, in the final section of the *reng*, a return is made to the mode and melodic ideas of the *darāmad* area.

For the analysis of a *reng*, one for *dastgāh-e Māhur*, by Qolām Hoseyn Darviš, has been chosen.[3] We shall examine this piece in terms of its relationship to *dastgāh-e Māhur* (refer to chapter 14).

This *reng* has sixty-six measures, and is in four sections (example 333, p. 192).

Section I   Measures 1–23, in the mode of *Māhur* (*darāmad*s) containing three phrases:

a.   Six measures (1–6): 1 and 2 are introductory measures, simply stating the finalis. The phrase actually begins with measure 3. Five and 6 are repetitions of 3 and 4, an octave lower. The phrase (m. 3) begins on the 5th above and ends with the 2nd above. The basic rhythmic pattern is: ♫♩ ♫♩ ‖.

b.   Five measures (7–11). Measures 7 and 8 are the same as 9 and 10, except for the substitution of a rest at the beginning of 7 for the tone of the finalis at the beginning of 9. The range of the phrase is a fourth (2nd below to 3rd above). The ending is on the finalis. The basic rhythmic pattern is: ♫♩ ♫♩♩│♩ ♪ ♪ ♩ ‖.

c.   Twelve measures (12–23). Measures 12, 13 and 14 are repeated sequentially, at a step lower, in measure 15, 16 and 17, and again at two steps lower in measures 18, 19 and 20. Measures 21, 22 and 23 are identical with measures 9, 10 and 11 (phrase 'b'). The ending is on the finalis. The basic rhythmic pattern is: ٣· ♫♩ ♫♩♩│♩ ♪ ♪ ♩│♩ ♪ ♩ ♪ ‖ .

Section II   Measures 24–44, in the mode of *Dād*, containing five phrases:

a.   Five measures (24–8). The main modal individuality of *Dād* is in making the 2nd above the finalis of *Māhur* into the note of *šāhed* and *ist*. This note is by far the most emphasised tone in this phrase. Measures 24 and 25 are repeated in 27 and 28. Measure 26 is merely three repeated notes (the *šāhed*), and serves to offset the 6/8 metre with its 3/4 design ♪٧ ♩ ♩. The ending is on the 2nd above.

b.   Four measures (29–32). Here the 3/4 and 6/8 alternate regularly: ♫♫♫│♫♩ ♩. ‖ . The *šāhed* of *Dād* (2nd above) is still emphasised, and the ending is on that note, which is also the *ist*. Measures 31 and 32 are exact repetitions of 29 and 30, but at an octave lower.

c.   Three measures (33–5). This phrase also concludes on the *ist* of *Dād*. The range of the melodic line is larger than in the previous measures (4th below to 3rd above). The rhythm here is uniformly 6/8: ♫♩ ♫♩ ‖.

d.   Four measures (36–9). The length of this phrase is actually two measures which are repeated an octave lower. The ending is on the *ist* of *Dād*, and the rhythm is the same as in phrase 'c'.

e.   Five measures (40–4). This phrase marks a return of emphasis on the finalis of *Māhur*, which is the last note, and is identical with phrase 'b' of section I. We see, then, that this phrase acts as a *forud* to *Māhur*, even though *Dād* does not constitute a decisive move away from *Māhur*.

Section III   Measures 45–55, in the mode of *Delkaš*, containing two phrases:

a.   Six measures (45–50). In order to create the mode of *Delkaš*, the 5th above the finalis of *Māhur* becomes a new finalis and the 6th above the finalis of *Māhur* is lowered by a microtone. This phrase ends on the new finalis, and is actually four measures but the last two of these (47 and 49) are repeated at an octave higher. The range of the phrase is that of a fourth. The rhythm is 6/8: ٧· ♫ ♫♩│♩ ♪ ♩ ♪ ‖.

b.   Five measures (51–5). Here the melodic line is extended to the 5th above the finalis of *Delkaš*. The ending is on the finalis. Rhythmically, this phrase is unusual; measures 53 and 54 are, in terms of points of stress and inner order, more correctly three measures of 2/4. They are certainly not in 6/8, but can be written in 3/4. In 3/4, the rhythm is ♫ ♩ ♫ | ♩ ♫ ♩ ‖ . In 2/4, it would be ♫ ♩ | ♫ ♩ | ♫ ♩ ‖ , which seems to be more natural to the implied accents of the line.

Section IV Measures 56–66, constituting a return and a *forud* in *Māhur*, contain two phrases:

a.   Six measures (56–61). This phrase begins with the 6th above the finalis of *Māhur*, which is returned to its original form. It is composed of material taken from phrases 'c' and 'a' of section I. Measures 56 and 57 are the same as 12 and 13; measures 58 and 59 are the same as 15 and 16; and measures 60 and 61 are the same as 3 and 4.
b.   Five measures (62–6). This phrase is an exact repetition of phrase 'b' of section I.

We see, therefore, that section IV is a brief version of section I, but with a somewhat different organisation. The form of the composition, as a whole, is A B C A. A is in the mode of *Māhur*, B in *Dād*, and C in *Delkaš*. Since the mode of *Dād* does not deviate from *Māhur* as much as *Delkaš*, section C represents a more distinct move away from A than does B.

The use of a *reng* as the concluding piece in a performance of a *dastgāh* is more commonly adhered to than the use of a *pišdarāmad* as the overture. Even in a solo performance, a *reng* is usually chosen to end the presentation. In ensemble playing, it is always used as the final number. In a vocal rendition of a *dastgāh*, however, a *tasnif* may take the place of the *reng*. Still, it would not be uncommon to have the *tasnif* followed by a *reng*.

Tasnif

The history of *tasnif* seems to parallel that of the *reng*. While there is a limited number of old *tasnif*s whose composers are not known, the great majority of them are of recent origin and have known composers. The term *tasnif* is loosely applied to any kind of vocal ballad. In the classical tradition, these songs are based on the poetry of the old masters, and on those of the more distinguished of the contemporary poets. Another genre of *tasnif*, with which we shall not be concerned here, corresponds to the popular ballad in the western countries, and employs poetry of poor quality by lesser contemporary poets. Although still more or less based on the modes of the classical music, this latter type of *tasnif* is usually sung by itself, and not as the ending piece for a *dastgāh*. The term *tarāne* is commonly used to define this type of modern and popular *tasnif*.

The overall design of the classical *tasnif* resembles that of *pišdarāmad* and *reng*. Again the mode of the *dastgāh*, for which the *tasnif* is composed, is established at the beginning and is brought back at the end. In the middle section or sections, one or more of the *gušes* of that *dastgāh* are brought to attention by the use of appropriate modal and melodic ideas.

Rhythmically, the *tasnif* is flexible and can be based on duple, triple or quadruple metres. The tempo can be slow to moderate and very seldom fast. The text is treated syllabically, except for occasional ornamentations on notes which, without embellishment, will be too long. This type of ornamentation is analogous to the western vibrato, which is not employed in Persian singing.

In the following, we shall give the analysis of a *tasnif* composed by Ali Naqi Vaziri for *dastgāh-e Abuatā*[4] (refer to chapter 5).

This *tasnif* has forty-four measures of 6/8 and is in three sections (Example 334, p. 191).

Section I   Measures 1–16, in the mode of *Abuatā*, containing two 4-measure phrases, making eight bars which are repeated:

a.   Four measures (1–4 and 9–12). The phrase begins on the *ist* (2nd above) of *Abuatā* and ends on the finalis. The melodic formation takes place between the 2nd and the 5th above; the finalis is heard only once at the end of the phrase, which corresponds exactly to a typical *Abuatā* phrase (*darāmads*). The first three measures are clearly 6/8, but the last measure has a 3/4 pattern: ♫ ♫ ♩ ‖.

b.   Four measures (5–9 and 13–16). This phrase has the same range as phrase 'a', but begins on the *šāhed* (5th above) and ends on the finalis. In both phrases, the area of concentration has been from the 2nd to the 5th above the finalis. Should the same two phrases be shifted a step lower, so that the emphasis is placed on the area of the finalis to the 4th above, instead of *Abuatā*, the atmosphere of *Šur* would be created. Thus, although the mode of *Abuatā* is considered to be a derivative of *Šur*, the difference between the two is unmistakable. Rhythmically, the two phrases are alike; phrase 'b' also ends with a 3/4 measure.

Section II   Measures 17–32, in the mode of *Hejāz*, containing two 4-measure phrases, repeated:

a.   Four measures (17–20 and 25–8). This phrase begins with a leap of a 5th from the finalis to the 5th above which is characteristic of a *Hejāz* melody (see phrase II of example 40, p. 37). After the leap of a 5th, the phrase employs only the tones from the 4th to the 8th above. The 5th above is the *šāhed* and the *ist*. Another peculiarity of *Hejāz*, the momentary raising of the 6th above by a half-step, is noted in the third measure of this phrase (m. 19). Rhythmically, this phrase does not deviate from 6/8 metre.

b.   Four measures (21–4 and 29–32). This phrase begins on the *šāhed* and ends on the 4th above. The range is from the 3rd to the 7th above. By bringing back the 3rd and the 4th, which were absent in phrase 'a', the way is paved for a return to the mode of *Abuatā*. The last measure of this phrase is in a 3/4 pattern, as was the case with the two phrases of section I.

Section III   Measures 33–44, in the mode of *Abuatā*, containing three phrases of section I.

a.   Four measures (33–6). With this phrase the mode of *Abuatā* is brought back. The 5th above is no longer the *šāhed*; it is the 4th above which has taken that function. The phrase begins on the 3rd and ends on the 2nd above (*ist* of *Abuatā*); the highest note is the 6th above. Rhythmically, the pattern of three measures of 6/8 followed by one of 3/4, as established in section I, is the rule in this section.

b.   Four measures (37–40). This phrase begins as a sequence of phrase 'a', at a lower step, but the sequential imitation is not maintained throughout. The range is from the finalis to the 5th above. The last two measures are the same as the last two measures of phrase 'b' of section I, except for the last note.

c.   Four measures (41–4). With the same range as phrase 'b', this phrase concludes on
       the finalis and uses the same ending measure as phrase 'b' of section I. Although
       sections I and III are not identical, the use of this ending measure in both sections
       helps to create greater unity in the piece.

Čahārmezrāb

A *čahārmezrāb* differs from *pišdarāmad*, *reng* and *tasnif*, both in function and in form. Unlike
the above three forms, a *čahārmezrāb* is not an ensemble piece but is a composition intended to
display the virtuosity of the solo performer. It is much in the nature of an instrumental *étude*;
it is a monothematic piece, the melodic basis of which is brief, often limited to a mere scale
pattern.

The rhythmic basis of a *čahārmezrāb* is usually a brief and constant pattern which, when
played rapidly, can create much excitement. Compound duple meter (6/8 and 6/16) is the
most common metric structure for a *čahārmezrāb*, but simple duple and triple meters are also
used.

As with *reng* and *tasnif*, there is a limited number of traditional *čahārmezrāb*s in use today
which date back to the nineteenth century and possibly before. Also, a large repertoire of
čahārmezrāb has come into use in recent decades, composed by contemporary musicians.

The traditional *čahārmezrāb*s are usually short, and admit a certain degree of improvisation
within the established rhythmic pattern. This improvisation is in the order of repeating
phrases, or building melodic sequences on the existing phrases. The new repertoire of
*čahārmezrāb*s, which are works of known musicians, are often lengthier and more pretentious
than the traditional *čahārmezrāb*s. Since they are composed and written, they are generally
performed without alterations through improvisation.

The role and the place of a *čahārmezrāb* is not at all clear. Within the same *dastgāh*, more
than one *čahārmezrāb* can be played. A *čahārmezrāb* can come at the very beginning of the
performance of a *dastgāh*, before the *darāmad*s, after the *pišdarāmad* or in place of a *pišdarāmad*. It may be placed in the midst of the *darāmad*s. After the *darāmad*s, one or more
*čahārmezrāb*s may be placed between some of the *guše*s of that *dastgāh*, in which case a
čahārmezrāb employing melodic ideas from the *guše* preceding or following is chosen. A
čahārmezrāb may also be placed before the *reng* or as a substitute for it. Accordingly, within
the repertoire of *čahārmezrāb*, there are those which are based on the mode of the *darāmad*s of
a *dastgāh*, and there are those which relate to the mode of the more singular *guše*s of the *dastgāh*.

The contemporary instrumentalist tends to intersperse his rendering of a *dastgāh* with an
ever-increasing number of *čahārmezrāb*s, some of which may be his own compositions. It
seems that a by-product of westernisation has been a growing interest in display pieces as
opposed to the more contemplative improvisatory pieces of the traditional music.

In one of its most common types, the *čahārmezrāb* establishes a rhythmic pattern which is
repeated identically in every measure. One or more of the notes in the pattern remains
constant throughout much of the piece, assuming the role of a pedal point. The note or notes
which change from one measure to the next move in an ascending or descending scale-wise
pattern. This simple movement provides a melodic basis for the piece which is often a mere
outline of a particular mode. The name *čahārmezrāb*, which may be translated as four strokes,
may in fact refer to this four-note melodic pattern.[5]

For the purposes of analysis, we have selected a *čahārmezrāb* of this type belonging to *guše-ye Hesār* of *dastgāh-e Čahārgāh* (refer to chapter 10). This is a traditional piece and has no known composer.[6] It has twenty-eight measures of 6/16, containing two parts (example 335, p. 192):

a.   Measures 1–15. This part establishes the 5th below the finalis of *Hesār* (which is at the same time the finalis of *Čahārgāh*) as the pedal point. The melodic movement begins with measure 3 and follows a four-note descending and ascending pattern, creating five short phrases. The range is from the 3rd below to the 4th above. The rhythmic structure is based on uniform measures of ♫♫♫ .

The melodic basis for this part can be reduced to the formula shown in example 336.

Example 336

b.   The second part is a continuation of the first, using the same melodic and rhythmic patterns, but shifts the line one step higher, so that the range is from the 2nd below to the 6th above. This part also contains five short phrases. Its melodic basis can be reduced to the formula shown in example 337.

Example 337

We see, therefore, that this type of *čahārmezrāb*, when reduced to its bare melodic minimum, is very simple and uninteresting. The interest lies in the way that the melody is embellished, and in the difficulty that, as a fast piece, it may pose to a performer.

The *čahārmezrāb* which we have just discussed can be played in any mode. The pedal point must be either the finalis or the *šāhed*, or another prominent tone in that mode. The choice will be made according to which one of these possibilities is provided by one of the low open strings on the instrument (*tār*, *setār*, *kamānde* or violin). The example we have just seen, in *Hesār* of *Čahārgāh*, makes use of the low string of the *tār* or the *setār* as the pedal point (the notation has been based on a *tār* performance), which, for *dastgāh-e Čahārgāh*, is tuned to c.

For purposes of comparison, we give, in example 338 (p. 192) the same *čahārmezrāb* as played in *dastgāh-e Šur*.[7]

Closing statement

Until the advent of modern communication media (recordings, radio, television and cinema), Persian classical music was within the reach only of a comparative few: the elite of urban society. Today, daily contact with music is within the experience of all citizens. The classical tradition is both limited in expression and too refined in character to satisfy the needs of mass entertainment. The response to contemporary needs has been found in the development of a genre of popular-commercial music. In this new music, modal schemes from the *dastgāh*s are blended with melodic and rhythmic features of western light music. Since the classical tradition is flexible and allows much freedom to the composer/performer, it becomes relatively easy to dilute it with elements which are essentially foreign to it. There is ample evidence, in fact, to indicate that the authenticity of this music is already compromised.

The foregoing is the substance of what I had written as a 'Concluding Statement' to my thesis when it was submitted in 1965. As I now reflect on the extraordinary events of the last quarter of a century, I must necessarily have a somewhat different conclusion. Up to 1979, the sweep of westernisation, and with it the growth and popularity of commercial music, was greatly accelerated. Since the revolution of 1978–9, however, not only has the process of westernisation been reversed, but virtually all musical activity has been brought to a halt.

Currently, Persia is run by an Islamic clerical regime of fundamentalist persuasions. The Islamic clerics have always had a proscriptive attitude towards music. The fact that music moves and affects the listener is inexplicable and, as such, suspicious. Furthermore, music is often viewed as an adjunct to merriment and self-indulgence, which are abhorred by the devout in all faiths.

If in 1965 there was reason to fear the gradual distortion of Persian music through westernisation, now there is reason to wonder if the tradition is to survive at all. In today's Persia, public musical life is non-existent, save for the so-called 'revolutionary' music which is in the service of the ideology of the state. All traditional musicians who were sustained through employment in radio and television, and as teachers at various schools, are out of work and are suffering intolerable deprivation. The harm that such dismal conditions have done to a musical tradition which does not rely on written symbols, and must be performed in order to live, is incalculable. The fate of Persian music – Persian culture, for that matter – may be determined solely by political events to an extent never experienced before.

It is against such a bleak prognostication that I am hopeful of having rendered a service, through this book, to the perpetuation of the splendid cultural heritage of my native land.

Appendix

Example 6, *Šur: Darāmad*

Example 9, *Šur: Zirkaš-e Salmak*

Example 11, *Šur: Salmak*

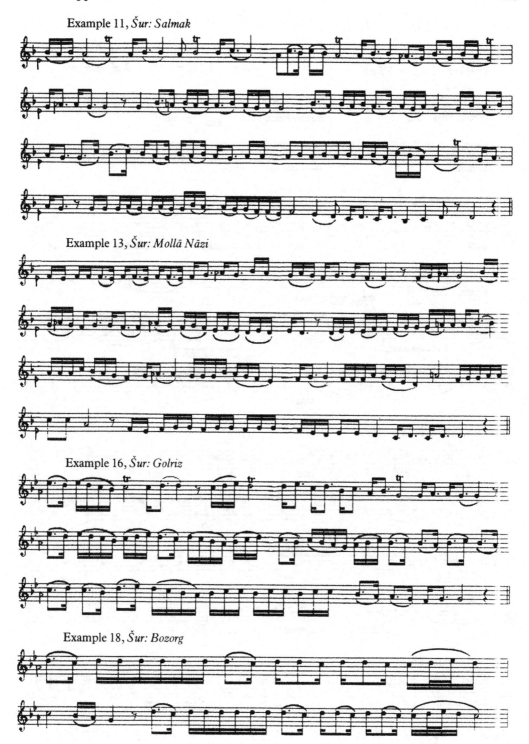

Example 13, *Šur: Mollā Nāzi*

Example 16, *Šur: Golriz*

Example 18, *Šur: Bozorg*

Continued overleaf

Example 18 *continued*

Example 20, *Šur: Xārā*

Example 21, *Šur: Qajar*

Example 23, *Šur: Ozzāl*

Example 25, *Šur: Šahnāz*

Example 27, *Šur: Qarače*

Continued overleaf

Example 27 *continued*

Example 29, *Šur: Hoseyni*

Example 32, *Šur: Bayāt-e Kord*

Example 33, *Šur: Gereyli*

Example 36, *Abuatā: Darāmad*

Example 38, *Abuatā: Sayaxi*

Example 41, *Abuatā: Hejāz*

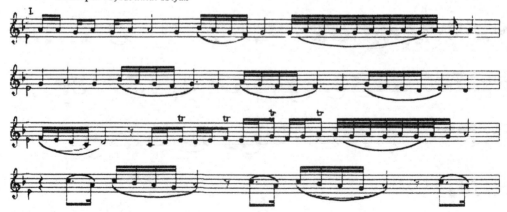

Example 42, *Abuatā: Čahār Bāq*

Continued overleaf

Example 42 *continued*

Example 44, *Abuatā: Gabri*

Example 47, *Dašti: Darāmad 1*

Example 48, *Dašti: Darāmad 2*

Example 50, *Dašti: Bidagāni*

Example 52, *Dašti: Čupāni*

Example 54, *Dašti: Daštestāni*

Example 56, *Dašti: Qamangiz*

Example 58, *Dašti: Gilaki*

Example 60, *Dašti: Kučebāqi*

Continued overleaf

Example 60 *continued*

Example 62, *Dašti: Oššāq*

Example 66, *Bayāt-e Tork: Darāmad*

Example 68, *Bayāt-e Tork: Dogāh*

Continued overleaf

Example 68 *continued*

Example 71, *Bayāt-e Tork: Ruholarvāh*

Example 73, *Bayāt-e Tork: Mehdizarrābi*

Example 75, *Bayāt-e Tork: Qatār*

Continued overleaf

Example 75 *continued*

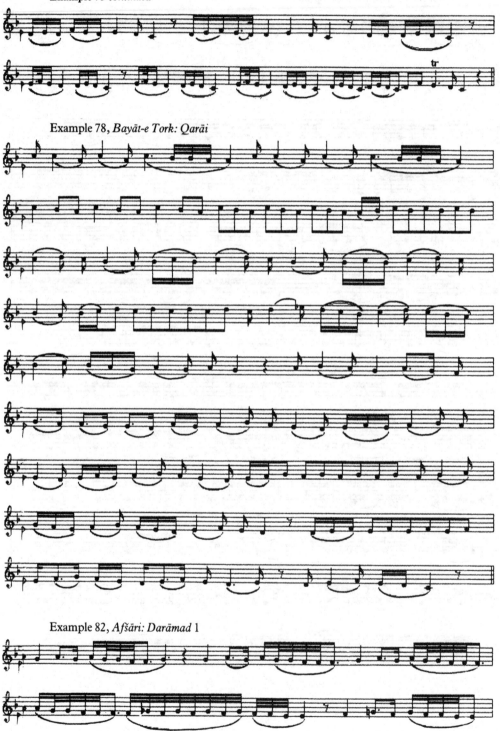

Example 78, *Bayāt-e Tork: Qarāi*

Example 82, *Afšāri: Darāmad 1*

Example 84, *Afšāri: Darāmad 2*

Example 86, *Afšāri: Rohāb*

Example 88, *Afšāri: Masihi*

Example 92, *Segāh: Darāmad*

Example 94, *Segāh: Zang-e Šotor*

Example 96, *Segāh: Zābol*

Example 98, *Segāh: Muye*

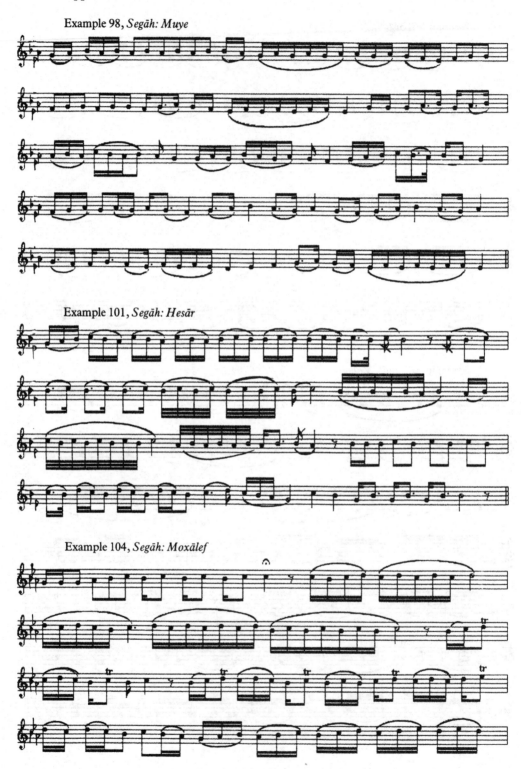

Example 101, *Segāh: Hesār*

Example 104, *Segāh: Moxālef*

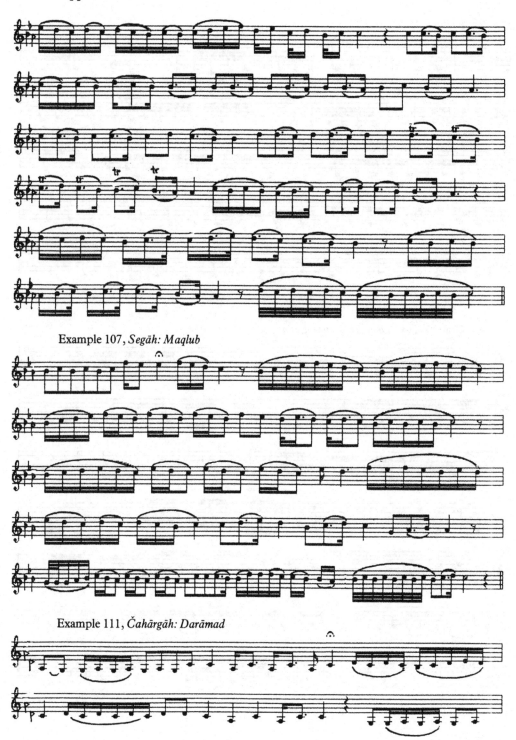

Example 107, *Segāh: Maqlub*

Example 111, *Čahārgāh: Darāmad*

Continued overleaf

Example 111 *continued*

Example 113, *Čahārgāh: Zang-e Šotor*

Example 115, *Čahārgāh: Zābol*

Example 118, *Čahārgāh: Muye*

Example 121, *Čahārgāh: Hesār*

Example 124, *Čahārgāh: Moxālef*

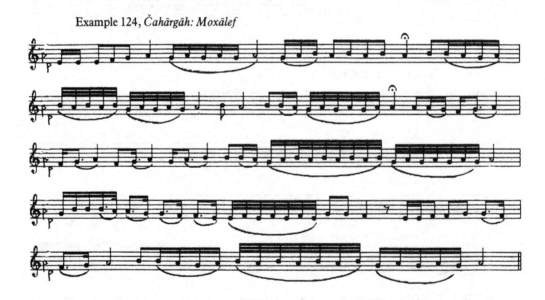

Example 127, *Čahārgāh: Maqlub*

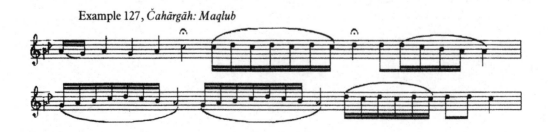

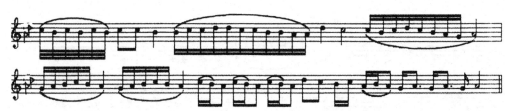

Example 130, *Čahārgāh: Hodi*

Example 133, *Čahārgāh: Pahlavi*

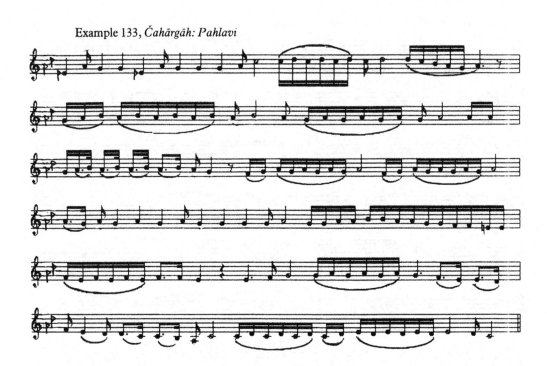

Example 135, *Ćahārgāh: Rajaz*

Example 138, *Ćahārgāh: Mansuri*

Example 144, *Homāyun: Darāmad*

Example 147, *Homāyun: Čahārgāh*

Example 149, *Homāyun: Movāliān*

Example 152, *Homāyun: Čakāvak*

Example 154, *Homāyun: Abolčap*

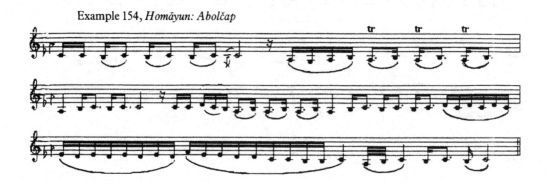

Example 156, *Homāyun: Tarz*

Example 158, *Homāyun: Leyli-o Majnun*

Example 161, *Homāyun: Bidād*

Continued overleaf

Example 161 *continued*

Example 163, *Homāyun: Ney Dāvud*

Example 166, *Homāyun: Nōruz-e Xārā*

Example 168, *Homāyun: Nafir*

Example 171, *Homāyun: Bayāt-e Ajam*

Example 175, *Homāyun: Šuštari*

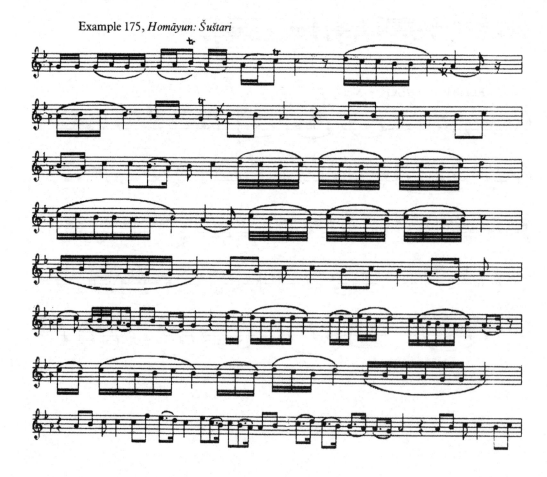

Example 180, *Homāyun: Baxtiāri*

Example 183, *Homāyun: Moālef*

Continued overleaf

Example 183 *continued*

Example 189, *Bayāt-e Esfahān: Darāmad*

Example 192, *Bayāt-e Esfahān: Bayāt-e Rāje'*

Example 196, *Bayāt-e Esfahān: Šāhxatāi*

Continued overleaf

Example 196 *continued*

Example 198, *Bayāt-e Esfahān: Suz-o Godāz*

Example 202, *Navā: Darāmad*

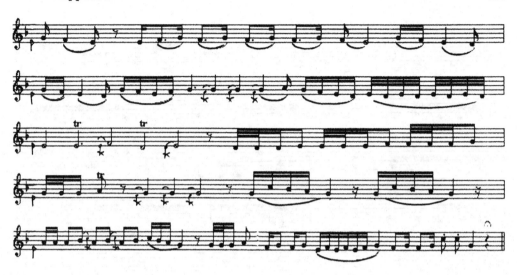

Example 204, *Navā: Gardāniye*

Example 207, *Navā: Nahoft*

Example 210, *Navā: Gavešt*

Example 212, *Navā: Neyšāburak*

Example 214, *Navā: Xojaste*

Continued overleaf

Example 214 *continued*

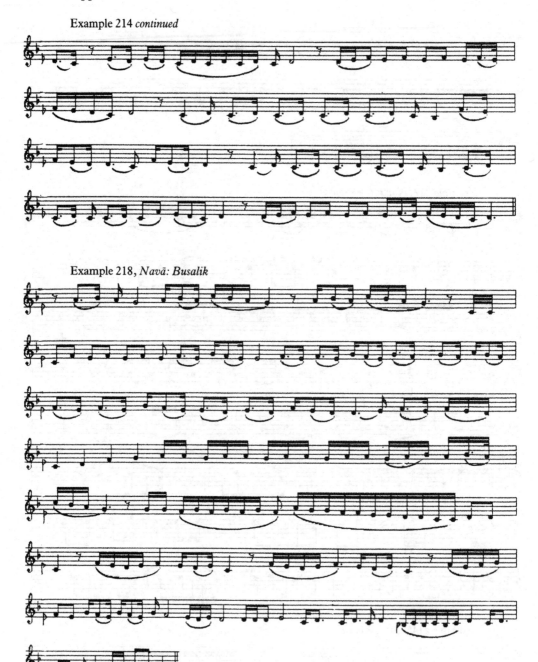

Example 218, *Navā: Busalik*

Example 221, *Navā: Neyriz*

Example 223, *Navā: Rahāvi*

Continued overleaf

Example 223 *continued*

Example 226, *Navā: Nāqus*

Example 229, *Navā: Taxt-e Tāqdis*

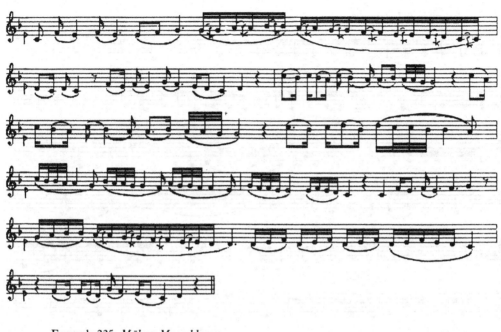

Example 235, *Māhur: Moqaddame*

Example 237, *Māhur: Darāmad*

Continued overleaf

Example 237 *continued*

Example 240, *Māhur: Dād*

Example 242, *Māhur: Xosrovāni*

Example 244, *Māhur: Tusi*

Example 246, *Māhur: Āzarbāyejāni*

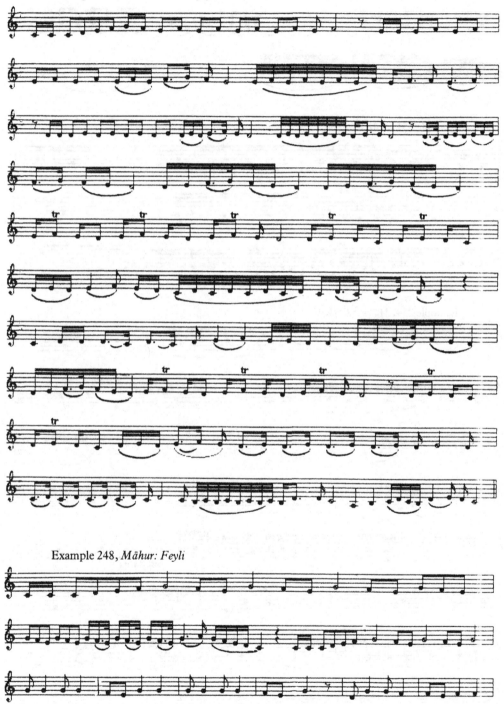

Example 248, *Māhur: Feyli*

Continued overleaf

Example 248 *continued*

Example 251, *Māhur: Abol*

Example 254, *Māhur: Delkaš*

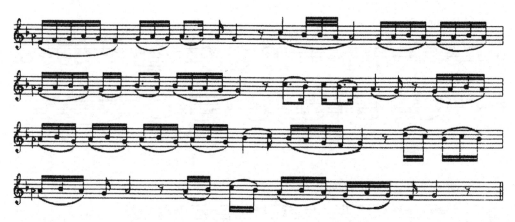

Example 258, *Māhur: Šekaste*

Continued overleaf

Example 258 *continued*

Example 261, *Māhur: Nahib*

Example 262, *Māhur: Arāq*

Example 265, *Māhur: Ašur*

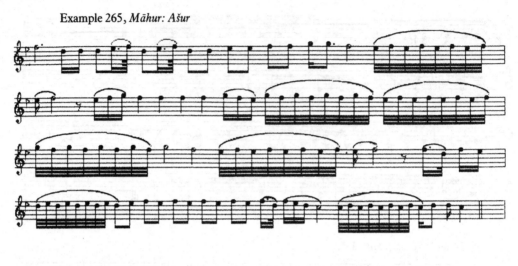

Example 267, *Māhur: Rāk*

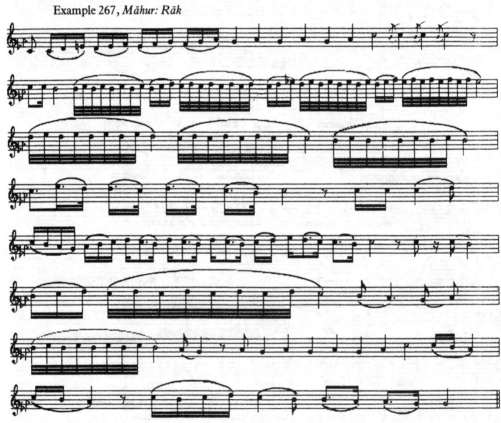

Example 269, *Māhur: Rāk-e Kašmir*

Example 271, *Māhur: Rāk-e Hendi*

Example 278, *Rāst: Darāmad*

Continued overleaf

Example 278 *continued*

Example 280, *Rāst: Parvāne*

Example 283, *Rāst: Ruhafzā*

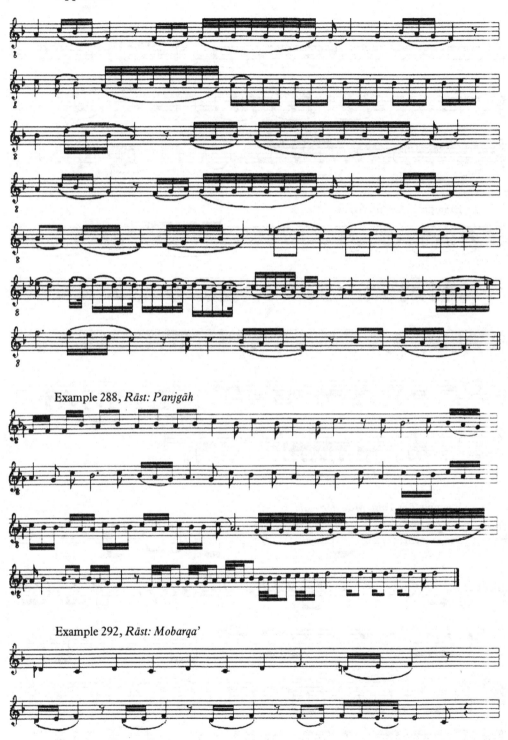

Example 288, *Rāst: Panjgāh*

Example 292, *Rāst: Mobarqa'*

Continued overleaf

Example 292 *continued*

Example 294, *Rāst: Sepehr*

Example 299, *Rāst: Māvarāonnahr*

Example 301, *Kerešme* in *Šur*

Example 302, *Kerešme* in *Bayāt-e Tork*

Example 303, *Kerešme* in *Segāh*

Continued overleaf

Example 303 *continued*

Example 304, *Kerešme* in *Hesār* of *Segāh*

Example 305, *Kerešme* in *Čahārgāh*

Example 306, *Kerešme* in *Maqlub* of *Čahārgāh*

Example 307, *Kerešme* in *Homāyun*

Example 308, *Kerešme* in *Bayāt-e Esfahān*

Example 309, *Kerešme* in *Arāq* of *Rāst*

Example 310, *Kerešme* in *Navā*

Example 311, *Bastenegār* in *Hejāz* of *Abuatā*

Example 312, *Bastenegār* in *Zābol* of *Čahārgāh*

Example 313, *Bastenegār* in *Afšāri*

Example 314, *Naqme* in *Rāst*

Example 315, *Naqme* in *Maqlub* of *Segāh*

Example 316, *Naqme* in *Abol* of *Māhur*

Example 317, *Zangule* in *Māhur*

Continued overleaf

Example 317 *continued*

Example 318, *Zangule* in *Čahārgāh*

Example 319, *Dotāyeki* in *Hesār* of *Čahārgāh*

Example 320, *Hazin* in *Navā*

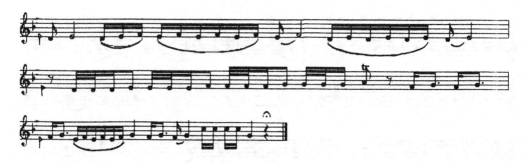

Example 321, *Hazin* in *Arāq* of *Navā*

Example 322, *Hazin* in *Šur*

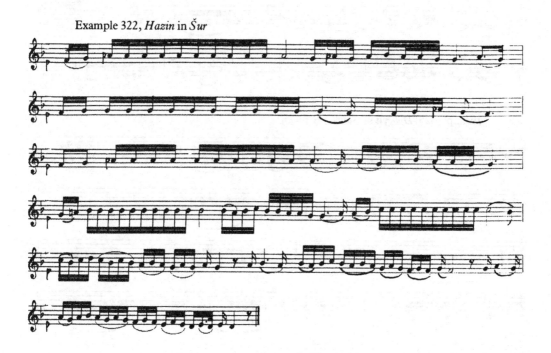

Example 323, *Hazin* in *Maqlub* of *Čahārgāh*

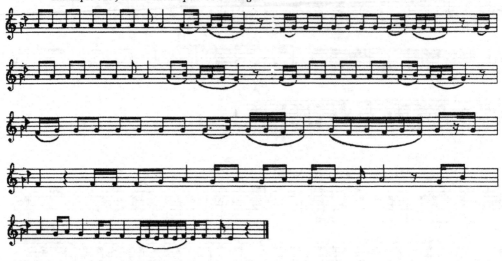

Example 324, *Dobeyti* in *Abuatā*

Example 325, *Dobeyti* in *Bayāt-e Esfahān*

Example 326, Beginning of *Jāmedarān* in *Afšāri*

Example 327, Beginning of *Jāmedarān* in *Homāyun*

Example 328, *Jāmedarān* in *Bayāt-e Esfahān*

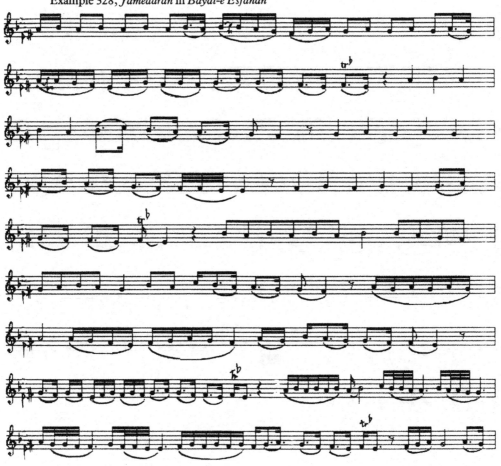

Continued overleaf

Example 328 *continued*

Example 329, *Masnavi Pič of Afšari*

Example 330, Beginning of *Masnavi* in *Šur*

Example 331, *Masnavi* in *Bayāt-e Esfahān*

Continued overleaf

Example 331 *continued*

Example 332, *Pišdarāmad in Homāyun* N. Zarrinpanje

Example 333, *Reng* in *Māhur* G. H. Darviš

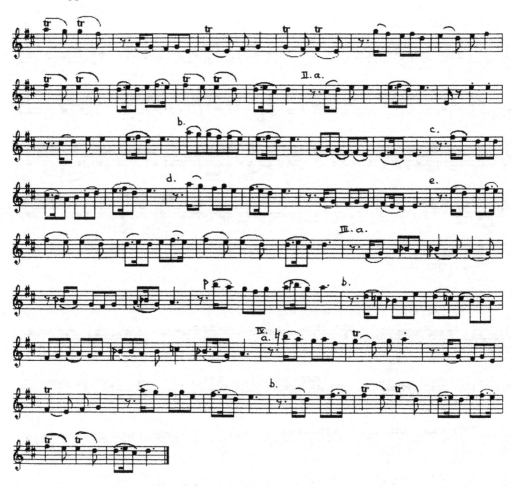

Example 334, *Tasnif in Abuatá*   A. N. Vaziri

Continued overleaf

Example 334 *continued*

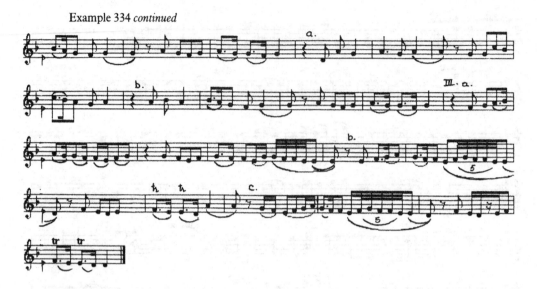

Example 335, *Čahārmezrāb* in *Hesār* of *Čahārgāh*

Example 338, *Čahārmezrāb* in *Šur*

Notes

1 A brief historical perspective

1 Xāleqi, *Nazari be Musiqi*, pp. 19–20.
2 Christensen, *L'Iran Sous les Sassanides*, p. 484.
3 Barkešli, *La Musique Traditionelle de l'Iran*, p. 2.
4 Engel, *Music of the most Ancient Nations*, p. 163.
5 Barkešli, *La Musique Traditionelle de l'Iran*, p. 4.

4 Dastgāh-e Šur

1 By tradition, four secondary *dastgāh*s, *Abuatā, Dašti, Bayāt-e Tork*, and *Afšāri* are considered as satellites of *Šur*. The matter will be discussed later as those *dastgāh*s are individually considered. Some Persian musicians even regard *Navā* as a derivative of *Šur*.
2 Vaziri, *Musiqi-ye Nazari*, p. 28.
3 Ma'rufi and Barkešli, *La Musique Traditionelle de l'Iran*.
4 In contemporary instrumental performances, in keeping with the general breakdown of traditional ways, the order of presentation of *guše*s from low to high register is no longer rigidly maintained.

5 Dastgāh-e Abuatā

1 This statement excludes 'modern' improvisations on such instruments as the violin or *santur*, where the display of virtuosity necessitates the use of a wide range.

8 Dastgāh-e Afšāri

1 Vaziri, *Musiqi-ye Nazari*, p. 41.
2 Xāleqi, *Nazari be Musiqi*, pp. 140–4.

9 Dastgāh-e Segāh

1 Xāleqi, *Nazari be Musiqi*, p. 194.

11 Dastgāh-e Homāyun

1 In *Rāst* the same rhythmic formula makes use of the 5th above and the finalis.
2 The practical range of most Persian instruments is from about f below middle c, to g an octave and a fifth above middle c.
3 Among instruments common to the classical tradition only the *santur* can comfortably provide notes down to d below middle c.
4 Elsewhere, the term *Bayāt* identifies a *dastgāh* (*Bayāt-e Tork* and *Bayāt-e Esfahān*) or an important *guše* (*Bayāt-e Raje'*).

12 Dastgāh-e Bayāt-e Esfahān

1 Vaziri, *Dastur-e Tār*, p. 105.
2 Vaziri, *Dastur-e Tār*, p. 105.

13 *Dastgāh-e Navā*

1 Vaziri, *Musiqi-ye Nazari*, p. 149; Xāleqi, *Nazari be Musiqi*, pp. 152–5.
2 Vaziri, *Musiqi-ye Nazari*, p. 151, states that *Gavešt* constitutes a modulation to *Segāh*. We believe that it can be a pivot for such a modulation. Its own melodic style, however, is not the same as that of a *Segāh darāmad*.

14 *Dastgāh-e Māhur*

1 Vaziri, *Musiqi-ye Nazari*, p. 68, states that 'The scale of *Māhur* is, without any difference, that of the major scale.'
2 Vaziri, *Musiqi-ye Nazari*, p. 68, states the opinion that the process of climbing to the *ōj* is no longer strictly followed, because that approach 'creates monotony'.
3 Xāleqi, *Nazari be Musiqi*, p. 158.
4 In *dastgāh-e Afšāri*, *Nahib* is concluded with a *forud* pattern of that *dastgāh*, and in *Navā*, a *forud* of *Navā* terminates the *Nahib*.

15 *Dastgāh-e Rāst (Rāst-Panjgāh)*

1 Vaziri, *Musiqi-ye Nazari*, p. 165.

16 Vagrant *gušes*

1 Both Vaziri and Barkešli have called the derivative *dastgāhs* (*Abuatā*, *Dašti*, *Bayāt-e Tork*, *Afšāri* and *Bayāt-e Esfahān*) by the name *naqme*, which means 'melody' or 'note'. This is a very different usage from the above application of the word. Furthermore it does not correspond with contemporary tradition, which calls the derivative *dastgāhs* by the name *āvāz* (song).
2 Ma'rufi and Barkešli, *La Musique Traditionelle de l'Iran*.
3 *Masnavi* is the metric basis for a certain type of Persian verse, e.g. the collection of *Masnavi* by Jalāleddin Rumi.

17 Compositional forms

1 *Violon*, Book 2, p. 42.
2 A very old type of *reng*, dating to the early nineteenth century, is *reng-e Šahrāšub*.
3 *Violon*, Book 2, p. 36, was originally composed for the *tār*. The transcription used here is the 'key' of D which is the most common key for *dastgāh-e Māhur* when played on the violin. For *tār* and *setār*, as we have seen, this *dastgāh* is unusually performed in the key of C.
4 Vaziri, *Dastur-e Jadid-e Tār*, p. 156.
5 This is the most reasonable speculation on the meaning of this term, as no one seems to know any other basis for this title.
6 Taken from *Dastgāh-e Čahārgāh*, Ma'rufi and Barkešli, *La Musique Traditionelle de l'Iran*, p. 17.
7 *Dastgāh-e Šur*, Ma'rufi and Barkešli, *La Musique Traditionelle de l'Iran*, p. 20.

Bibliography

The following list is not exhaustive, but contains the titles cited in the text together with other major works on the subject.

Amir-Jāhed, Mohammad Ali, *Divān-e Amir-Jāhed*, Tehran: Majles Press, 1954
Archer, William Kay (ed.), *The Preservation of Traditional Forms of the Learned Music of the Orient and the Occident*, Urbana: University of Illinois Institute of Communications Research, 1964
Barkešli, Mehdi, *L'Art Sassanide Base de la Musique Arabe*, Tehran: Presses Universitaires, 1947
  'La gamme de la musique Iranienne', *Annales des Télécommunications*, 5 (May, 1947)
  'La musique iranienne' in Roland Manuel (ed.), *L'histoire de la Musique: Encyclopédie de la Pléiade*, vol. IX, Paris: Pléiade, 1960, pp. 455–523
Beeman, William O, 'You can take the music out of the country, but . . .: the dynamics of change in Iranian musical tradition', *Asian Music*, 7:2 (1974), 6–19
Caron, Nelly, 'The Ta'zieh, the sacred theatre of Iran', *The World of Music*, 17:4 (1975), 3–10
Caron, Nelly and Dariouche Safvate, *Iran: les Traditions Musicales*, Paris: Buchet/Chastel, 1966
Caton, Margaret, 'The vocal ornament *takiyah* in Persian music', *UCLA Selected Reports in Ethnomusicology*, 2:1 (1974), 42–53
  'The classical *tasnif*: a genre of Persian vocal music', unpublished Ph.D dissertation, University of California at Los Angeles, 1983
Christensen, Arture E., 'La vie musicale dans la civilisation des Sassanides', *Association Française des Amis de l'Orient, Bulletin* (April–October, 1936)
  L'Iran Sous les Sassanides, Copenhagen: E. Munksgaard, 1944
D'Erlanger, Rodolphe von, *La Musique Arabe*, 5 vols., Paris: Librarie Orientaliste, Paul Gaunthner, 1930–59
Dastur-e Moqaddamāti-ye Tār va Setār, Publication of Anjoman-e Musiqi-ye Melli (National Music Society), Tehran: Ferdowsi Press, 1951
During, Jean, 'Music, poetry and visual arts in Persia', *The World of Music*, 1 (1982), 72–88
  La Musique Iranienne, Tradition et Evolution, Editions Recherches sur les Civilisations, Paris, 1984
  'La musique traditionelle iranienne en 1983', *Asian Music*, 15: 2 (1984), 11–31
Engel, Carl, *The Music of the Most Ancient Nations*, 2nd edn, London: William Reeves Bookseller Ltd, 1929
Farhat, Hormoz, *The Traditional Art Music of Iran*, Tehran: Ministry of Culture and Arts Press, 1973
  'Iran', in Stanley Sadie (ed.), *The New Grove Dictionary of Music and Musicians*, London: MacMillan, 1980
Farmer, Henry G., 'An outline of history of music and musical theory', in Arthur Upham Pope (ed.), *A Survey of Persian Arts*, vol. III, London: Oxford University Press, 1939
  Studies in Oriental Musical Instruments, Glasgow: Civic Press, 1939
  'Music of Islam', *The New Oxford History of Music*, vol. I, *Ancient and Oriental Music*, London: Oxford University Press, 1957
Forsat-Dole, Mirza Naser, *Bohur el Alhan*, Shiraz. 1903. Revised edn, Bombay, 1913
Forutan-Rād, Ahmad, *Tarānehā-ye Jādid*, Tehran: Elmi Press, 1937
Gerson-Kiwi, Edith, *The Persian Doctrine of Dastga-Composition: a Phenomenological Study in Musical Modes*, Tel Aviv: Israel Music Institute, 1963

Hedāyat, Mehdi Qoli, *Majmaol Advār*, parts I, II and III, Tehran, 1928

Hejdah Qat'e Pišdarāmad, edited by Lotfollāh Mofaxxam-Pāyān. Tehran: Ferdowsi Press, 1956

Khatschi, Khatschi, *Der Dastgah, Studien zur neuen persischen Musik*, Kolner Beitrage zur Musikfor-schung, vol. XIX, Regensburg: Gustave Bosse Verlag, 1962

   'Das Intervallbildungsprinzip des persischen *Dastgah Shur*', *Jahrbuch für musikalische Volks- und Völkerunde* 3 (1967), 70–84

Khoshzamir, Mojtaba, 'Aspects of the Persian tasnif', University of Illinois, unpublished M.M. thesis, 1975

   'Ali Naqi Vaziri and his influence on music and music education in Iran', University of Illinois unpublished doctoral dissertation, 1979

Klitz, Brian, and Norman Cherlin, 'Musical acculturation in Iran', *Iranian Studies* 4 (1971), 157–66

Ma'rufi, Musā, *Čahārgāh: Pišdarāmad, Tasnif va Reng*, Tehran, 1932

   Avāz-e Dashti, Tehran, 1948

Ma'rufi, Musā and Mehdi Barkešli, *La Musique Traditionelle de l'Iran*, Tehran: Majles Press, 1963

Mahmoud, Parviz. 'A theory of Persian music and its relation to western practice', unpublished doctoral dissertation, University of Indiana, 1957

Majale-ye Musiqi (Music Journal), monthly publication of the Ministry of Fine Arts, Tehran, July 1956–August 1965

Massoudieh, Mohammad Taghi, *Awaz-e Sur*, Regensburg: Bosse, 1968

   'Die melodie Matnawi in der persischen Kunstmusik', *Orbis Musicae* (Tel-Aviv) 1:1 (1971), 57–66

   'Die Musikforschung in Iran', *Acta Musicologica*, 48 (1976), 65–85

   'Hochzeitslieder aus Balucestan', *Jahrbuch für musikalische Volks- und Völkerkunde* 7 (1973), 58–69

   'Tradition und Wandel in der persischen Musik des 19. Jahrhunderts', in R. Günther (ed.), *Musikkulturen Asiens, Afrikas und Ozeaniens im 19. Jahrundert*, Regensburg: Bosse (1973), pp. 73–94

   Radif vocal de la musique traditionelle de l'Iran, Tehran: Vezārat-e Farhang va Honar, 1978

Modir, Hafez. 'Research Models in Ethnomusicology Applied to the Radif Phenomenon in Iranian Classical Music', *Pacific Review of Ethnomusicology* 3: 63–78, 1986.

Mofaxxam-Pāyān, Lotfollāh, *Bist-o Panj Qat'e-ye Zarbi*, Tehran: Ferdowsi Press, 1948

Nettl, Bruno. 'Attitudes towards Persian music in Tehran, 1969', *Musical Quarterly* 56 (1970), 183–97

   'Notes on Persian classical music of today: the performance of the *Hesar* section of *Dastgah Chahar-gah*', *Orbis Musicae* (Tel-Aviv) 1:3 (1972), 175–92

   'Nour-Ali Boroumand, a twentieth-century master of Persian music', *Studia Instrumentorum Musicae Popularis* 3 (1974), 167–71

   'Persian popular music in 1969', *Ethnomusicology* 16 (1974), 218–39

   'Thoughts on improvisation, a Comparative Approach', *Musical Quarterly* 60 (1974), 1–19

   'Musical values and social values: symbols in Iran', *Journal of the Steward Anthropological Society* 10:1 (1978), 1–23

   'Some aspects of the history of world music in the twentieth century: questions, problems, concepts', *Ethnomusicology* 22: 123–36, 1978c.

   The Radif of Persian Music, Studies of Structure and Cultural Context. Elephant and Cat. Champaign, Illinois, 1987.

Nettl, Bruno with Béla Foltin, Jr, *Daramad of Chahargah: a Study in the Performance Practice of Persian Music*, Detroit: Detroit Monographs in Musicology, no. 2, 1972

Nettl, Bruno and Daryoosh Shenassa, 'Towards a comparative study of Persian radifs: focus on *Dastgah-e Mahour*', *Orbis Musicae* (Tel-Aviv) 8 (1983), 29–43

Nettl, Bruno and Amnon Shiloah, 'Persian classical music in Israel: a preliminary report', *Israel Studies in Musicology* 1 (1978), 142–58

Saba, Abolhassan, *Qateāt-e Zarbi Barāye Violon*, Tehran: Ferdowsi Press, 1946

   Dore-ye avval-e [dovvom-e, sevvom-e čahārom-e] santur, Tehran: no publisher (originally published in the 1950s), *c.* 1965

Dore-ye avval-e [dovvom-e, sevvom-e] violon, Tehran: no publisher (originally published in the 1950s), *c*. 1967

Dore-ye avval-e tār va setār, Tehran: no publisher (originally published in the 1950s), *c*. 1970

Sabā, Hoseyn, *Xodāmuz-e Santur*, Tehran: Ferdowsi Press, 1956

Sadeghi, Manoochehr, 'Improvisation in nonrhythmic solo instrumental contemporary Persian art music', unpublished MA thesis, California State College at Los Angeles, 1971

Tsuge, Gen'ichi, 'Rhythmic aspects of the Avaz in Persian Music', *Ethnomusicology* 14 (1970), 205–27

'A note on the Iraqi maqam', *Asian Music* 4:1 (1972), 59–66

'Avaz: a study of the rhythmic aspects in classical Iranian music', unpublished Ph.D dissertation, Wesleyan University, 1974

Vaziri, Ali Naqi, *Dastur-e Tār*, Berlin: Kāviāni Press, 1922 (?)

Dasture-e Violon. Tehran, 1933

Musiqi-ye Nazari, part II, Tehran: Tolu' Press, 1934

Dastur-e Jadid-e Tār, Tehran, 1936

Violon, books I, II, III and IV, publication of Honarestān-e Musiqi-ye Melli (Conservatory of National Music), Tehran: Ferdowsi Press, 1952

Wright, Owen, *The Modal System of Arab and Persian Music AD 1250–1300*, London: Oxford University Press, 1978

Xāleqi, Ruhollāh, *Nazari be Musiqi*, Tehran: Aftāb Press, 1938

Sargozašt-e Musiqi-ye Irān, vols. I and II, Tehran: Ferdowsi Press, 1954

Zonis, Ella, 'Contemporary art music in Persia', *Musical Quarterly* 51 (1965), 638–48

'Classical Persian music today,' in Ehsan Yar-Shater (ed.), *Iran Faces the Seventies*, (New York: Praeger), 1971, pp. 365–79

Classical Persian Music: an Introduction, Cambridge, Mass: Harvard University Press, 1973

Index

CPSIA information can be obtained at www.ICGtesting.com
Printed in the USA
LVOW03s0420160915

454271LV00017B/549/P